Lazy Baking

For Hen,

Here's to many
creative adventures
ahead together!

Thank you for everything.
Crispbreads and wine,
here we come,

Love Den

Lazy Baking

Really easy sweet and savoury bakes

JESSICA ELLIOTT DENNISON

Hardie Grant

BOOKS

Contents

INTRODUCTION
PAGE 8

BAKING BASICS
PAGE 23

MORNING
PAGE 50

MID-MORNING
PAGE 74

LUNCH
PAGE 100

AFTERNOON
PAGE 122

EVENING
PAGE 140

ABOUT JESS
PAGE 170

ABOUT ELLIOTT'S
PAGE 171

INDEX
PAGE 172

I'M A HOME COOK. SO WHEN IT COMES TO BAKING, MY APPROACH MEANS MINIMAL FUSS, YET COMFORTING AND DELICIOUS.

Introduction

MINIMAL FUSS, MORNING, NOON, AND NIGHT

In the pages ahead you'll find realistic guidance for baking in my relaxed style throughout the day.

There are Porridge Soda Bread Rolls (page 52), Yoghurt Flatbreads (page 54) and One-Cup Pancakes (page 67) for slow weekends; there are zesty Soft Amaretti (page 80) and bright Lemon Earl-Grey Polenta Loaf (page 84) to enjoy with coffee on busy mornings; you'll find rustic Tomato, Parmesan and Caper Galettes (page 104) to throw together with a quick salad for satisfying mid-week lunches; there are jam-filled Thumbprint Cookies (page 94) and spiced Sugar Buns for Tea (page 132) to tuck into on rainy afternoons; and I've got foolproof cakes and galettes you can rely on for last-minute surprises and celebrations. There are also stress-free desserts like my one-pan Elliott's Flourless Chocolate Cake (page 162) and an impressive yet foolproof Hazelnut and Brown Sugar Pavlova (page 156) for whipping up when friends come over. I've even included salty, garlicky, ridiculously easy Baked Crispbreads (page 142) to make a well-deserved bottle of Friday-night wine that bit more special.

I've developed my One-Jar Peanut Butter Cookies (page 126) using only four ingredients so that you can bake them in a few minutes – ideal for those moments when you just need a quick-fix treat using what's already in the cupboard. I've also tested, tweaked and re-tested the most-loved recipes from my Edinburgh kitchen space, Elliott's. My top-sellers, Pork and Fennel Sausage Rolls (page 102), Elliott's Sea Salt Chocolate Cookies (page 116), Sticky Triple Ginger Cake (page 131) and Marmalade Sourdough Pudding (page 160) have all been simplified, ensuring you'll get incredible results in your own kitchen, no matter your confidence or baking experience.

HOME BAKING ON SCIENNES ROAD

In the summer of 2018 I opened Elliott's, a kitchen and shop on Sciennes Road in Edinburgh (an interesting street name for a Londoner like me to pronounce correctly). The concept was pretty straightforward; I'd cook a relaxed weekly menu following the seasons, alongside offering simple bakes, good coffee and interesting wines. I'm at my happiest when cooking for friends and loved ones, so Elliott's was to be essentially an extension of my own small kitchen at home: an excuse to feed people and make it my job.

Within just a few months, Elliott's transformed into a magical community space. There's something special about the place, quietly tucked behind Edinburgh's leafy meadows with the golden light that hits our south-facing, apple-green walls. Enthusiastic locals want to have proper chats with us and their neighbours here. So that, combined with the smell of whatever is in the oven wafting down Sciennes Road, makes Elliott's a real place of optimism.

You get a sense along Sciennes Road of how the community might have felt in years past. Our customers pause from their busy days and their focus turns to sipping coffee on the bench while enjoying a cookie or a slice of Sticky Triple Ginger Cake (page 131). Phones and endless newsfeeds are abandoned for a quiet moment in favour of a nice conversation, even sometimes with a stranger. Being part of a neighbourhood like this is an immensely satisfying feeling, even with those 5 a.m. alarm calls on Scotland's darkest winter mornings.

REALISTIC RECIPES FOR EVERYDAY LIFE

These are the trusted recipes I use most often in my busy life. So, as with my previous books, expect minimal ingredients (that are all easy to find), standard kitchen kit, little need for washing up, plus lots of ideas for adapting recipes to make them seasonally relevant.

You'll spot there's an emphasis on fruit when it's at its best and most affordable, plus store-cupboard items like miso paste, fennel seeds, tahini and sea salt, along with plenty of citrus zest to bring interest, brightness and flavour to the bakes rather than tooth-aching sweetness.

COMMUNITY-TESTED RECIPES

Along with friends from the Elliott's Instagram community who live further afield, many of our Sciennes Road customers have kindly tested the recipes in this book in their own kitchens. I started the process of compiling the recipes in March 2020, during the first lockdown, when sharing baking experiences felt like the best way to connect with our Edinburgh community. Blind testing every recipe ensures the steps and methods I provide offer consistent, delicious finished results, so I owe a big, warm thank you to everyone who offered their time and invaluable feedback.

ADAPTING TO TINY KITCHENS

After turning on the coffee machine each morning, the first task for my small team at Elliott's is to get the oven hot before baking a rotation of trays of amaretti, cookies, loaf cakes, galettes, crumbles, pastries and sausage rolls. There are usually a few marinated chickens and pumpkins competing for oven space, too, in time for the lunch rush! It's somewhat of a dance as we operate from a tiny kitchen with a single and often temperamental oven.

Much like my kitchen at home in the Scottish Borders, there's minimal worktop and fridge space at Elliott's and certainly no room for any fancy kit. Ultimately, both my kitchens at work and home have led me to develop into the laziest of bakers. If one of our recipes has seven steps, I'll do whatever I can to streamline it to three or four without compromising the end results. Likewise, if I can get a delicious outcome from throwing everything into one mixing bowl or pan rather than three (the Elliott's Flourless Chocolate Cake on page 162, for example), then that's what I'll do.

In the pages ahead, I've done all the hard work so you can enjoy the same reliable bakes in your own home as I do in both my little but well-loved kitchens. Presenting the special people in your life with a big pot of coffee and something warm, comforting and sticky from the oven, without any fuss, is surely one of life's simplest pleasures.

Happy baking,
Jess

KIT FOR LAZY BAKING

I've really tried to keep equipment to a minimum as that's how I bake both at home and at Elliott's. The recipes that follow don't require anything out of the ordinary. Gather together a set of scales, a whisk, a couple of large bowls, a wooden spoon, a couple of baking sheets, a loaf and/or cake tin, a set of measuring spoons, an ovenproof dish, a grater and some non-stick baking paper and you'll be good to go. Hopefully you've accumulated most of these items already, but if not, they're readily available and don't require a huge investment.

Balloon whisk vs electric whisk

In order to get the best results from a recipe, please note the differences between a balloon whisk and an electric whisk.

By balloon whisk I mean the old-fashioned type; a set of wires that loop into a bulb-like shape at one end. A balloon whisk helps to increase the amount of air that you can whip into your cake batters.

A handheld electric whisk is super useful for creaming butter and sugar together (in the Elliott's Sea Salt Chocolate Cookies recipe on page 116, for example) as well as egg whites (in the Soft Amaretti recipe on page 80 and the Hazelnut and Brown Sugar Pavlova recipe on page 156). However, an electric whisk can overwork a cake batter where I've specified to use a balloon whisk. I'm all for making life easier, but for best results, don't be tempted to speed things up by swapping a balloon whisk for an electric whisk unless I've suggested it, as you might overwork your bake.

So much love for my food processor, but you don't need one!

My parents generously bought me a small Magimix food processor for my 18th birthday – the poor thing has been in constant use ever since. Initially, I used it for the occasional hummus, soup or curry paste in my early dinner-party experimentation phase (cringe!), but now I use it daily at Elliott's for making batches of Salted Chocolate-Hazelnut Spread (page 63) and Marmalade Sourdough Pudding (page 160), as well as endless rounds of aioli. I should probably invest in something more 'professional' as visiting chefs are always shocked at the lack of 'pro' kit in the Elliott's kitchen. But, along with my mum's 1980's faded red lemon juicer that we use for hundreds of lemons each week, I've grown very attached to my small food processor.

Please don't worry if you don't own a food processor. I now don't have one at home, as I'm yet to replace the one I took to Elliott's on the first day of trading. For the handful of recipes that use one, I've suggested using a more affordable hand blender: they often come with a neat whisk attachment too. For the handful of recipes that suggest a food processor, I've included guidance for a work-around, using shop-bought ground almonds instead of grinding your own in the Basic Frangipane recipe on page 45, for example.

Thoughts on eggs, butter, milk and vanilla

I prefer to use medium-sized, free-range eggs for baking, but don't worry if you've only got small or large eggs to hand. The recipes are pretty flexible and a few grams more or less of egg here or there isn't going to ruin anything.

Likewise, it doesn't matter if you've got salted or unsalted butter in your kitchen; both are fine in all the recipes. I prefer whole or full-fat milk for its delicious creaminess, but again, skimmed milk will still work out great.

Proper vanilla isn't cheap but I really recommend investing in good-quality pods or beans, paste or extract and using it sparingly. Request some the next time you're asked for gift ideas, perhaps? Cheaper versions of vanilla *essence* will save you some cash, but you'll really notice a cheaper, more synthetic, manufactured taste that could potentially ruin your baking efforts.

Store-cupboard heroes

When snooping around my friend's fridges and cupboards
to research how they shop and cook (sad to admit, but it's deeply
fascinating!), I've found most of us tend to have half-used and often-
forgotten jars of miso paste and tahini, along with unused spices
that were purchased for a one-off recipe.

Therefore, you'll notice I introduce these savoury heroes into
quite a few of the baking recipes, giving them a new lease of life in
something sweet; for example, garam masala to spice the Sticky
Triple Ginger Cake (page 131) and fennel seeds to flavour my Fennel
Seed and Lemon Pastries (page 70).

Miso paste is another lazy hack of mine; it offers a long-ferment
sourdough-like vibe to the quick brunch Yoghurt Flatbreads
(page 54). Although not technically baking as such, I couldn't not
include my Miso-Honey Almond Butter (page 63) for spreading on
toast as it's pretty special. There's a whole beautiful world of miso
and the products vary in colour, flavour and taste. Don't worry about
finding a particular type though, just use whatever is to hand or
easiest to get hold of. And if you can't find miso, simply substitute it
with a good pinch of sea salt flakes. Maldon is my favourite sea salt.

Shop-bought puff pastry

I love the ease of making galette pastry, so much so that it's one of my Baking Basics (page 39). But sometimes you can't beat the convenience of a shop-bought puff pastry, especially the ready-rolled sheets that mean you don't even need to reach for a rolling pin.

Don't be surprised to see me recommending shop-bought puff pastry for my mid-morning Fennel Seed and Lemon Pastries (page 70) and lunchtime Pork and Fennel Sausage Rolls (page 102). I look out for decent-quality, all-butter brands of pastry though, as they taste far nicer than any strange margarine or palm-oil kinds.

An obsession with citrus (and its zest), especially lemons

I admit it, be it lemon, grapefruit, orange or lime, I'm addicted to citrus. In our early days, Elliott's was often referred to as being 'the lemon cafe' and I'm quite alright about that.

You'll notice lemon is used in loads of the recipes as I love the freshness and vibrancy it brings, often cutting through the sweetness of other ingredients. Lemon zest especially offers balance and contrast in baking; I guess that's my cook's approach coming into play.

I find a Microplane grater is a brilliant investment for quickly zesting citrus, but if you don't have one, just use the side of a box grater with the smallest holes. The next time you need a last-minute present, I urge you to give the chocolate truffles with grapefruit zest a try (page 139). They're pretty magical, yet couldn't be easier to make.

Thoughts on oven temperature

Ovens work in mysterious ways, with each one heating differently no matter what the temperature display says. I've tested these recipes using a fan oven. If you are using a conventional oven, increase the heat by around 20°C. Use the chart at the back of the book on page 172 for extra guidance.

The recipes in this book are all pretty flexible, so a minute less or longer in the oven isn't going to ruin your efforts. I'd advise keeping an eye on things and, most importantly, following your instincts on when a cake feels ready or not, as it's this experience that will lead you to becoming a more confident baker. In-oven thermometers cost very little to buy online and can help eliminate any guesswork. The classic skewer test for checking whether the middle of a cake is fully baked never fails either – the skewer should come out clean.

Baking Basics

CUSTARD
JAM
PASTRY
FRANGIPANE

Custard, jam, pastry and frangipane provide the foundations for my approach to baking, whether sweet or savoury. Therefore, you'll notice me referencing each of them regularly throughout the main recipes in this book. Get to know the simple methods for my Baking Basics and they'll set you up nicely in the kitchen for years to come.

Custard

There's room for two types of custard in my life. First, the proper traditional kind that reminds me of school-dinner sponge puddings and mum's Sunday-lunch crumbles. Although it's not difficult to make, a traditional-style custard does take a few minutes of stirring, which is highly therapeutic, until it's perfectly thickened. So with this in mind, I've also developed a quicker custard hack that only takes five minutes to prepare. Think of this one as the younger cousin custard; bright and zesty thanks to the lemon and crème fraîche but with the familiarity of vanilla. It is ideal for swiftly satisfying a mid-week craving or, even better, throwing into the freezer where it transforms into an incredible no-churn ice cream.

PROPER TRADITIONAL CUSTARD

MAKES
570 ml (1 pint) – enough for 4–8 people (depending on how much of a custard nut you are) to go with a whole crumble, ginger cake or chocolate cake

TAKES
20 minutes

300 ml (10 fl oz/1¼ cups) double (heavy) cream
400 ml (13 fl oz/generous 1½ cups) milk (ideally whole/full-fat)
3 egg yolks (save the egg whites for the Soft Amaretti on page 80 or Hazelnut and Brown Sugar Pavlova on page 156)
45 g (1¾ oz/scant ¼ cup) caster (superfine) sugar
1 tablespoon cornflour (cornstarch)
1 teaspoon vanilla paste or 1 vanilla pod (bean), seeds scraped out
pinch of sea salt flakes

1   Pour the cream and milk into a large saucepan and heat over a medium heat, stirring occasionally, until bubbles start dancing on the surface. Remove from the heat before it begins to boil.

2   Meanwhile, using a balloon whisk or wooden spoon, beat the egg yolks, sugar, cornflour (cornstarch), vanilla paste or seeds and salt together in a large bowl until completely smooth.

3   Taking lots of care, pour a few splashes of the hot cream and milk mixture over the egg mixture, whisking all the time to ensure your eggs don't scramble.

4   Gradually pour the remaining hot cream and milk mixture into the eggs, continuing to whisk all the time.

5   Scrape clean the pan. Pour the custard mixture back into the pan and then heat over a very low heat, whisking regularly, for 10–15 minutes or until the custard is thickened to your liking. Make sure the custard doesn't stick to the base of the pan as this will prevent any lumps forming.

6   Transfer to a heatproof jug and enjoy hot or cold.

FIVE-MINUTE CRÈME FRAÎCHE CUSTARD

MAKES
enough for 4 people to go with pie, or for 2 people as ice cream (roughly 5–6 scoops)

TAKES
5 minutes

300 g (10½ oz) crème fraîche (ideally full-fat)
4 tablespoons caster (superfine) sugar
1 teaspoon vanilla paste
pinch of sea salt flakes
3 egg yolks (save the egg whites for the Soft Amaretti on page 80 or Hazelnut and Brown Sugar Pavlova on page 156)
grated zest of 1 lemon (optional)

1   Place all the ingredients in a medium saucepan and, using a balloon whisk, beat until completely smooth.

2   Place over the lowest heat and, stirring regularly, heat until warm. Make sure the custard doesn't stick to the base of the pan as this will prevent any lumps forming.

3   Transfer to a heatproof jug and enjoy hot or cold.

TIP

To make a No-Churn Ice Cream, make the custard following the instructions above but increasing the amount of sugar to 6 tablespoons. Transfer the custard to a metal tub or container. Freeze for at least 6 hours before serving.

Flavouring custard

Bay leaves, cinnamon bark, crushed cardamon pods, a few turns
of the peppermill, ground espresso powder and citrus peel are all
brilliant ways to infuse different flavours into the Proper Traditional
Custard (page 27).

Saving a split custard

Don't panic if you do get a few lumps or scrambled egg yolks at any
point when making custard. Just blitz the mixture in a food processor
or with a hand blender until smooth, or transfer to a cold bowl to stop
the custard overheating and pass it through a sieve (strainer)
to remove any lumps.

Making ice cream

Both the custards make incredible no-churn ice creams.
Or, try pouring them into ice-pop moulds for frozen treats.

Stabilising with cornflour

Cornflour (cornstarch) isn't an absolute must when making custard,
however it does help to stabilise the egg yolks and cream. You can
make the Proper Traditional Custard without cornflour, just ensure
things don't overheat, or you risk scrambling the eggs.

Make ahead

Both custards keep well in the fridge for up to 5 days.

JAM AND COCONUT SPONGE

PAGE 115

STICKY TRIPLE GINGER CAKE

PAGE 131

A CRUMBLE-HEAVY CRUMBLE

PAGE 150

MARMALADE SOURDOUGH PUDDING

PAGE 160

Jam

I'm fascinated by capturing seasonal fruit flavours in a jar, but jam making has a reputation for being a drawn-out, traditional process. With the rapid jam-making methods that follow, you can easily make a jar of jam using whatever fruit you have to hand.

STRAWBERRY AND LEMON JAM

MAKES
1 small jar (about 230 g/8 oz)

TAKES
10 minutes, plus cooling time

250 g (9 oz) strawberries, hulled and halved
75 g (2½ oz/⅓ cup) caster (superfine) sugar
grated zest of ½ lemon, plus 1 tablespoon juice

1   Put all the ingredients in a small saucepan and then, using a fork, crush half the strawberries.

2   Heat over a high heat until the mixture reaches a rapid boil. Let it boil for 6 minutes, stirring regularly with a spatula to ensure it doesn't catch on the base of the pan.

3   Carefully spoon the jam into a clean, sterilised jar, screw on the lid and allow to cool.

BLUEBERRY AND ROSEMARY JAM

MAKES
1 small jar (about 230 g/8 oz)

TAKES
10 minutes, plus cooling time

250 g (9 oz) blueberries
75 g (2½ oz/⅓ cup) caster (superfine) sugar
1 tablespoon lemon juice
1 sprig of rosemary, leaves only, finely chopped

1   Put all the ingredients in a small saucepan and then, using a fork, crush half the blueberries.

2   Heat over a high heat until the mixture reaches a rapid boil. Let it boil for 6 minutes, stirring regularly with a spatula to ensure it doesn't catch on the base of the pan.

3   Carefully spoon the jam into a clean, sterilised jar, screw on the lid and allow to cool.

APPLE AND CARDAMOM JAM

MAKES
1 small jar (about 230 g/8 oz)

TAKES
10 minutes, plus cooling time

2 small apples, peeled and roughly chopped
2 cardamom pods, husks removed, seeds crushed
pinch of sea salt flakes
75 g (2½ oz/⅓ cup) caster (superfine) sugar
thinly sliced peel and juice of ½ lemon

1   Put all the ingredients in a small saucepan with 40 ml (2½ tablespoons) water.

2   Heat over a high heat until the mixture reaches a rapid boil. Let it boil for 6 minutes, stirring regularly with a wooden spoon to ensure it doesn't catch on the base of the pan. Crush some of the apple chunks as they soften.

3   Carefully spoon the jam into a clean, sterilised jar, screw on the lid and allow to cool.

RHUBARB AND GINGER JAM

MAKES
1 small jar (about 230 g/8 oz)

TAKES
10 minutes, plus cooling time

1 stalk rhubarb, thinly sliced (forced rhubarb gives the best colour)
75 g (2½ oz/⅓ cup) caster (superfine) sugar
1 tablespoon lemon juice
½ teaspoon finely grated ginger

1   Put all the ingredients in a small saucepan.

2   Heat over a high heat until the mixture reaches a rapid boil. Let it boil for 6 minutes, stirring regularly with a wooden spoon to ensure it doesn't catch on the base of the pan.

3   Carefully spoon the jam into a clean, sterilised jar, screw on the lid and allow to cool.

NOTES ON JAM

Checking your jam is ready

The easiest way to test whether a jam is 'set' is to place a plate in the fridge while you make the jam. After the 6 minutes of cooking time, spoon a bit of jam onto the cold plate and then chill for a further 2 minutes. I prefer a soft-set jam, which means when you run your finger through it, the jam just about holds together without too much juice seeping. If the jams feels too runny or you prefer your jam hard-set, boil the mixture for a further few minutes and test it again.

Cleaning jars

I find the easiest way to sterilise a jam jar is to thoroughly wash the jar and lid, then sit them in a pan of boiling water while the jam cooks. Carefully drain and dry the jar with a clean tea towel before filling it with the hot jam.

Ensuring a tight seal

Once you've filled the jar with your cooked jam, screw on the lid then turn the jar upside down – the heat will create a vacuum that seals the lid. If the above tips on sterilising and sealing all sound like too much fuss, just keep the jam in the fridge and eat it quickly, before your jam has the chance to spoil.

EAT JAM WITH

PORRIDGE SODA BREAD ROLLS
PAGE 52

ONE-CUP PANCAKES
PAGE 67

THUMBPRINT COOKIES
PAGE 94

JAM AND COCONUT SPONGE
PAGE 115

Pastry

Galettes are a kind of free-form tart that feature heavily in my weekly cooking, both at home and Elliott's, as they're so relaxed yet satisfying. For the minimal effort this pastry recipe requires, you are rewarded with a flaky, buttery crust that serves as a base for whatever fruit and veg you have to hand. There's no worrying about lamination or precise shaping the dough, in fact, the rougher your galette, the more rustic and inviting it will end up looking.

BASIC PASTRY

MAKES
enough for 1 sweet or savoury tart,
serving 6 people

TAKES
5 minutes, plus 1 hour chilling time

150 g (5 oz/1¼ cups) plain
    (all-purpose) flour, plus extra
    for dusting
pinch of sea salt flakes
85 g (3 oz) cold butter (salted or
    unsalted), cut into cubes
1 teaspoon caster (superfine) sugar
    (if making pastry for a sweet tart,
    otherwise leave out the sugar for
    a savoury tart)

1   Rub the flour, salt and butter (plus sugar, if making sweet
    pastry) together in a large bowl, using your index and middle
    fingers and thumbs, until you've got large, rough flakes.
    (Don't worry if some of the butter remains quite chunky.)

2   Stir in a few splashes of cold water until the mixture is
    combined to a dough.

3   Wrap the dough in cling film (plastic wrap) or beeswax wrap
    and pop in the fridge for 1 hour or in the freezer for 30 minutes.

NOTES ON PASTRY

Keep that butter cold

The key to crisp, flaky pastry is to move quickly and not to overwork or to overthink the dough. Having large chunks of cold butter in your dough means you'll get lovely crisp layers of pastry. We're not aiming for silky smooth, glossy pasta dough here. For galettes, think rustic, lumpy dough.

Throw it on a pie

The Basic Pastry (page 39) is ideal for throwing over a pie dish filled with your favourite sweet or savoury filling. Roll out the dough to fit over your pie dish and then, using a fork, crimp the edges. Brush the pastry with egg wash before baking for a golden finish.

Get ahead with a batch in the fridge or freezer

When well-wrapped in cling film (plastic wrap) or beeswax wrap, galette dough will happily keep for up to three days in the fridge. It's also worth doubling up on the galette dough and throwing a portion in the freezer where it'll keep nicely for up to one month. Just allow the dough to fully defrost before rolling it out and you're good to go.

USE BASIC PASTRY FOR

APPLE FRANGIPANE GALETTE
PAGE 82

TOMATO, PARMESAN AND CAPER GALETTES
PAGE 104

CHICKEN CURRY PIE
PAGE 112

LEEK, BLUE CHEESE AND POTATO GALETTE
PAGE 146

Frangipane

Sounding fancier than it is, frangipane is simply a sweet, creamy, nutty paste for spreading over fruit galettes and filling tarts to make them extra special. It can also be spooned into sponge cakes and used to fill pastries. Essentially, whatever you make with frangipane will certainly be delicious – you really can't go wrong.

BASIC FRANGIPANE

MAKES
enough for 1 sweet galette,
serving 6 people

TAKES
5 minutes

50 g (2 oz) roasted whole almonds or
  ground almonds
30 g (1 oz) butter (salted or unsalted),
  soft/at room temperature
70 g (2½ oz/⅓ cup) sugar (ideally
  caster/superfine)
1 egg yolk (save the egg whites
  for the Soft Amaretti on page 80
  or Hazelnut and Brown Sugar
  Pavlova on page 156)
pinch of sea salt flakes
2 tablespoons cream or milk
  (ideally whole/full-fat)

Food-processor method
1   Using roasted whole almonds instead of ground almonds,
    blitz the almonds in a food processor until finely ground.

2   Add the butter, sugar, egg yolk, salt and cream or milk to
    the food processor and blitz again until fully combined.

Hand-mixer method
1   Using ground almonds instead of whole almonds, place
    the almonds, butter, sugar, egg yolk, salt and cream or milk
    in a large bowl.

2   Using an electric whisk or wooden spoon, beat all the
    ingredients together until fully combined.

Substitute different nuts

You can use whatever nuts you've got in the store-cupboard to make frangipane. Hazelnuts (filberts), pistachios and walnuts all work really well.

Use freshly roasted nuts

To give your frangipane a deeper, nuttier flavour, spread the nuts over a baking sheet and roast them in a 180°C fan (400°F/gas 6) oven, then leave them to cool completely before blitzing in a food processor.

Keep a batch in the fridge

Frangipane keeps nicely for a week if well covered, so you can make a batch and then reach for it at a later date to make something delicious.

USE FRANGIPANE FOR

FENNEL SEED AND LEMON PASTRIES
PAGE 70

APPLE FRANGIPANE GALETTE
PAGE 82

BLOB TEASPOONFULS INTO MY GO-TO BROWN SUGAR SPONGE
PAGE 128

Morning

PORRIDGE SODA
BREAD ROLLS
PAGE 52

YOGHURT FLATBREADS
PAGE 54

BAY AND RED WINE
BLACKBERRIES
PAGE 58

YORKSHIRE-PUDDING
PANCAKE
PAGE 60

SPREADS FOR TOAST
PAGE 63

ONE-CUP PANCAKES
PAGE 67

FENNEL SEED AND
LEMON PASTRIES
PAGE 70

Porridge Soda Bread Rolls

There's something incredibly homely and comforting about these rolls. Simply split in half, lightly toast, slather with an inch-thickness of butter and enjoy with a big pot of breakfast tea.

MAKES
8 rolls

TAKES
10 minutes, plus 25–30 minutes baking time

150 g (5 oz/1½ cups) rolled porridge oats, plus extra for sprinkling
250 g (9 oz/2 cups) plain (all-purpose) flour, plus extra for dusting
2 teaspoons bicarbonate of soda (baking soda)
1 teaspoon caster (superfine) sugar, brown sugar or honey
1 teaspoon sea salt flakes
1 egg
350 g (12 oz) plain natural yoghurt
splash of milk, for brushing (optional)

1   First, preheat your oven to 180°C fan (400°F/gas 6). Line a large baking tray (pan) with baking paper.

2   Next, place the oats, flour, bicarbonate of soda, sugar and salt in a large mixing bowl. Using a fork or balloon whisk, thoroughly mix together all the ingredients to ensure the bicarbonate of soda is evenly distributed. (Biting into a clump of raising agent is no fun!)

3   Make a small well in the middle of the dry ingredients. Crack the egg into this well and, using a fork or balloon whisk, mix the egg into the mixture. Pour in the yoghurt and then stir until it becomes a scruffy-looking dough.

4   Dust your work surface and hands with a few spoonfuls of flour and then, using your hands, gently knead the dough until combined. (You don't want to knead very much.)

5   Pat the dough into a rectangle measuring 25 x 15 cm (10 x 6 in), then divide into 8 equal-sized rolls. Rather than being perfectly circular, I prefer my rolls to be a rough triangle-ish shape, as shown opposite, but you do as you please!

6   Transfer the rolls to the lined baking tray. If using, gently dab the milk over the rolls with your fingers and then sprinkle a few extra oats onto each roll.

7   Bake for 25–30 minutes or until golden brown.

8   These rolls are best eaten on the day they're made, or they will keep until the next day when stored in an airtight container.

Yoghurt Flatbreads

MAKES
2 large or 4 small flatbreads (scale up the recipe accordingly to make more)

TAKES
15 minutes

Considering how good they taste, these pillowy flatbreads are ridiculously cheap and easy to make. The dough doesn't require any resting time, so you can whip them up in minutes. Plus, if you include the optional miso paste, you can hack the flavour of a long-fermented sourdough without any of the fuss of caring for a starter.

Here I've given ideas for using the flatbreads as sweet and savoury brunch options, but make the flatbreads for lunch and dinner too – they're great companions to dals, curries, kebabs, falafel, etc.

---

125 g (4 oz/1 cup) plain (all-purpose) flour, plus extra for dusting
½ teaspoon baking powder
125 g (4 oz) strained natural yoghurt
2 teaspoons white or brown miso paste (or ¼ teaspoon sea salt flakes if you don't have any miso in the fridge)
2 teaspoons cold-pressed rapeseed (canola), olive or vegetable oil

1   First, combine the flour and baking powder together in a large bowl to ensure the baking powder is evenly distributed. Stir through the yoghurt and miso or sea salt to make a dough.

2   Warm a large non-stick frying pan (skillet) over a high heat until it gets really hot and starts to smoke.

3   Meanwhile, tip the dough onto a lightly-floured work surface. Using your hands, knead the dough for 1–2 minutes or until smooth.

4   Divide the dough equally into two halves. Using a rolling pin dusted with flour, roll out each piece of dough into a flatbread measuring roughly 18 cm (7 in) in diameter.

5   Taking great care as the pan will now be incredibly hot, drizzle 1 teaspoon of the oil into the hot pan. Lay a flatbread in the pan and cook for 2 minutes on one side without moving it.

6   Using tongs, carefully flip the flatbread over and fry on the other side for a further 2 minutes, or until charred at the edges and puffing up in the middle. Transfer to a warm plate.

7   Reduce the heat to medium, add the remaining teaspoon of oil then repeat with the second flatbread.

WITH DILL-SCRAMBLED
EGGS AND YOGHURT

MAKES
enough for 2 flatbreads

TAKES
5 minutes

1 x quantity Yoghurt Flatbreads
    (opposite)
3 tablespoons cold-pressed rapeseed
    (canola) or olive oil
small bunch of dill (around 15 g/½ oz),
    coarsely chopped
5 eggs
½ teaspoon sea salt flakes
2 tablespoons strained natural yoghurt
1 lemon

1   First, make the flatbreads following the instructions
    on the page opposite.

2   Next, warm the oil in a separate large, non-stick frying pan
    (skillet) over a high heat. Working quickly, throw the dill into
    the pan and allow it to sizzle for 30 seconds or until fragrant.

3   Reduce the heat to medium and crack the eggs into the pan.
    Allow the eggs to sit for 1 minute while the whites start to cook.
    Throw in the salt and, using a spatula, gently fold the eggs
    a couple of times while cooking for a further 2 minutes, or until
    the eggs are gently cooked through.

4   Place a flatbread on each plate and divide the eggs between
    them. Spoon over the yoghurt and then, using a Microplane or
    the fine side of a box grater, finely zest the lemon over the eggs.

5   Cut chunky wedges from the lemon and serve alongside the
    flatbreads to squeeze the juice over the eggs before eating.

WITH CRUSHED CORIANDER SEEDS, HONEY AND FIGS

MAKES
enough for 2 flatbreads

TAKES
5 minutes

1½ teaspoons coriander seeds
1 x quantity Yoghurt Flatbreads
    (page 54)
1 teaspoon honey, plus 2 tablespoons
    for serving (or, even better, 2
    chunks of honey on the comb)
175 g (6 oz) strained natural yoghurt
5 ripe, fresh figs

1   First, crush the coriander seeds in a mortar with a pestle
    or using a rolling pin on your chopping board.

2   Make the flatbreads following the instructions on page 54,
    folding the crushed coriander seeds through the dough along
    with 1 teaspoon of the honey before kneading.

3   Place a flatbread on each plate. Spoon over the yoghurt and
    the extra honey or honeycomb. Tear the figs into rough pieces
    and scatter over the flatbreads.

WITH SAGE-FRIED EGGS AND LEMONY GREENS

MAKES
enough for 2 flatbreads

TAKES
10 minutes

1 x quantity Yoghurt Flatbreads
    (page 54)
4 tablespoons cold-pressed rapeseed
    (canola) or olive oil
12 sage leaves (kept whole and
    on stalks)
2 eggs
pinch of sea salt flakes
handfuls of trimmed cavolo nero
    or cabbage/any seasonal greens,
    coarsely chopped
zest and juice of ½ lemon (grate the
    zest on a Microplane or fine side
    of a box grater before juicing)

1   First, make the flatbreads following the instructions on page 54.

2   Next, warm 2 tablespoons of the oil in the pan you used for
    the flatbreads over a medium heat. Throw in the sage leaves
    and leave them to crisp up before pushing them to one side
    of the pan. Increase the heat to high, carefully crack the eggs
    into the pan and then, using a spatula or fish slice, flick the
    crispy sage leaves over the top of the eggs. Fry over a high heat
    until the egg whites are super-crisp on the outside, but the
    yolks are still a little runny (or done to your liking).

3   Season with plenty of salt and remove from the heat.

4   In a second pan, warm the remaining 2 tablespoons of oil over
    a high heat. Add the greens, lemon juice and a pinch of salt to
    the pan and fry over a high heat for 1 minute, or until wilted.

5   Place a flatbread on each plate. Divide the wilted lemony greens
    between the flatbreads and top each with a sage-fried egg.
    Splash over any sage-infused oil and finish with the lemon zest.

Bay and Red Wine Blackberries

MAKES
enough for 4 servings

TAKES
5 minutes, plus 40 minutes baking time

I find comfort in knowing there's something seasonal, bright and compote-y in the fridge for spooning over morning yoghurt, pancakes, or later in the day, over ice cream.

You can easily swap the blackberries for raspberries or strawberries if they're best at the moment. Stone fruit, apples or pears cooked with cider in a similar way is also delicious.

450 g (1 lb) blackberries (about 3 punnets)
4 bay leaves
50 g (2 oz/¼ cup) caster (superfine) sugar
6 turns of black pepper
100 ml (3½ fl oz/scant ½ cup) red wine

1   First, preheat the oven to 180°C fan (400°F/gas 6).

2   Toss the blackberries and bay leaves in the sugar in a 20 x 25-cm (8 x 10-in) baking tray (pan). Season the fruit with the freshly ground pepper and pour over the red wine. Cover the tray tightly with kitchen foil and then bake in the preheated oven for 20 minutes.

3   Remove the foil and bake for a further 15 minutes. If you prefer a thicker syrup with the berries, rather than a thin juice, spoon out the berries with a slotted spoon and pop the juices back in the oven for a further 5 minutes or until syrupy. Allow to cool before serving.

4   Thanks to the wine and sugar, these berries keep well in the fridge in an airtight container for up to one week, so they are ideal for spooning over the One-Cup Pancakes (page 67) and strained natural yoghurt.

Morning

Yorkshire-Pudding Pancake

MAKES
1 large pancake/to fill a 14-cm (5½-in) cast-iron pan (scale up the recipe accordingly to make more)

TAKES
5 minutes, plus 15 minutes baking time

Preheating your oven to high means this simple pancake batter will puff up in a similar way to a Yorkshire pudding or a popover, making a dramatic, brunch-table special. I've used blackcurrants here, but of course, feel free to use whatever berries you have. If you want to go all out, serve the pancake with maple syrup and bacon instead of the extra sugar and lemon juice.

1 egg
1 teaspoon caster (superfine) sugar, plus 1 teaspoon for sprinkling
50 ml (1¾ fl oz/3 tablespoons) milk (ideally whole/full-fat)
¼ teaspoon vanilla paste
40 g (1½ oz/⅓ cup) plain (all-purpose) flour
tiny pinch of sea salt flakes
grated zest of ⅓ lemon, plus ½ lemon for squeezing over
5 g (¼ oz) butter
handful of blackcurrants

1   First, preheat the oven to 220°C fan (475°F/gas 9) and place your cast-iron pan in the oven to warm for at least 5 minutes.

2   Meanwhile, using an electric whisk (or balloon whisk with plenty of elbow grease), mix together the egg, sugar, milk, vanilla, flour, salt and lemon zest in a large bowl until really fluffy.

3   Wearing oven gloves (mitts), carefully remove the hot pan from the oven. Add the butter to the pan, swirling it around so that the melted butter coats the base and sides.

4   Pour the batter into the pan and then scatter over the blackcurrants. Bake for 15 minutes or until golden and crisp on the edges. Don't be tempted to open the oven door as the pancake may collapse and flatten.

5   Wearing oven gloves again, remove the pan from the oven and transfer the pancake to a plate. Sprinkle the pancake with the extra sugar and squeeze over the lemon juice. Eat straight away.

Spreads for Toast

I know they're not technically baking as such, but these spreads have a very special place in my kitchen and I'm hoping they'll transform your morning toast too! (Just a heads up, you will require a small food processor to get the desired textures.)

SALTED CHOCOLATE-HAZELNUT SPREAD

MAKES
1 x 280-g (9¾-oz) jar

TAKES
10 minutes, plus 15 minutes baking time

100 g (3½ oz) blanched hazelnuts (filberts)
50 g (2 oz) dark (bittersweet) chocolate, broken into chunks
35 ml (1 fl oz) cold-pressed rapeseed (canola) oil or neutral-flavoured oil
50 g (2 oz) honey
25 g (1 oz) cocoa (unsweetened chocolate) powder
½ teaspoon sea salt flakes

1   First, preheat the oven to 200°C fan (425°F/gas 7).

2   Spread out the hazelnuts (filberts) over a large baking tray (pan) and toast in the oven for 15 minutes, or until golden and fragrant. Remove from the oven and leave to cool on the tray for a couple of minutes.

3   Transfer the toasted hazelnuts to a food processor along with the remaining ingredients. Blitz for 5–10 minutes or until smooth and glossy.

4   Using a spatula, transfer the spread to a clean, sterilised jar.

5   This spread keeps well in the fridge for up to 2 months. Enjoy with sourdough toast or One-Cup Pancakes (page 67).

MISO-HONEY ALMOND BUTTER

MAKES
1 x 300-g (10½-oz) jar

TAKES
10 minutes, plus 8–10 minutes baking time

200 g (7 oz) flaked (slivered) almonds
2½ tablespoons honey
3 tablespoons cold-pressed rapeseed (canola) oil or neutral-flavoured oil
1 tablespoon miso paste

1   First, preheat the oven to 200°C fan (425°F/gas 7).

2   Spread out the almonds over a large baking tray (pan) and toast in the oven for 8–10 minutes, stirring halfway through. Remove from the oven and leave to cool on the tray.

3   Transfer the toasted almonds to a food processor along with the remaining ingredients. Blitz for 5–10 minutes or until smooth, like a shop-bought nut butter. (How long this takes will depend on how powerful your food processor is.)

4   Using a spatula, transfer the nut butter to a clean, sterilised jar.

5   This nut butter keeps well in the fridge for up to 2 weeks.

One-Cup Pancakes

MAKES
10–12 pancakes (depending on the size of your cup!)

TAKES
10 minutes

You don't even need to get the weighing scales out to make these pancakes – simply grab a cup or mug and use it to roughly measure out the ingredients. Within minutes, you'll be enjoying light, fluffy pancakes. Serve them with strained natural yoghurt and any flavour jam (page 33) or spread (page 63) and a little grated citrus zest, or your own favourite toppings.

1 egg
1 level cup self-raising flour
1 cup milk (either dairy milk or a plant-based milk)
pinch of sea salt flakes
1½–2 knobs (pats) of butter (salted or unsalted)

1   First, crack the egg into a large mixing bowl. Using a cup or mug, measure out the level cup of flour and add it to the bowl. Repeat with the milk and then throw in the salt. Using a balloon whisk, mix together all the ingredients until you have a fairly smooth batter.

2   Next, warm a large non-stick frying pan (skillet) over a high heat. Add half a knob (pat) of butter to the pan and heat until bubbling, swirling it around so that the melted butter coats the base and sides.

3   Spoon 2 tablespoons of batter into the pan to form a small pancake. Continue spooning in more batter – you'll probably fit 3 or 4 pancakes in your pan at once, but make sure there's plenty of space between them as it'll make flipping them easier. Cook fewer pancakes at a time, if necessary.

4   Cook the pancakes on one side for 1–2 minutes then, using a spatula or fish slice, carefully flip them over and cook for a further minute on the other side until nicely golden. (You may need to reduce the heat to medium if the pan is getting too smoky.) Transfer to a plate.

5   Add another knob of butter to the pan and continue to make more pancakes until you've used up all the batter.

Fennel Seed and Lemon Pastries

MAKES
12 small pastries

TAKES
25 minutes, plus 35–40 minutes baking time

Fennel seeds aren't just for pasta, curries or sprinkling over sausage rolls (although they are very tasty on them, see page 102). Here, the pops of aniseed that the fennel seeds offer magically combine with sweet, sticky frangipane and lemon zest to transform shop-bought puff pastry into something that tastes far more sophisticated than it is.

Yes, I'm aware that asking you to zest three lemons might sound extreme for a single batch of pastries, but it's the citrus zest that really makes these, trust me.

---

1 sheet ready-rolled all-butter puff pastry (about 35 x 23 cm / 14 x 9 in)
1½ tablespoons icing (confectioner's) sugar

Fennel seed and lemon frangipane
50 g (2 oz/½ cup) ground almonds
30 g (1 oz) butter, soft/at room temperature
70 g (2½ oz/scant ⅓ cup) caster (superfine) sugar
1 tablespoon honey
1 egg yolk (save the egg white for the Soft Amaretti on page 80 or Hazelnut and Brown Sugar Pavlova on page 156)
pinch of sea salt flakes
2 tablespoons milk (ideally whole/full-fat), plus 1 tablespoon for brushing
1½ tablespoons fennel seeds, plus 1 tablespoon for sprinkling
grated zest of 2 lemons, plus 1 lemon for zesting after baking (save the juice from the lemons for making any of the jam recipes on page 33)

1   First, preheat the oven to 180°C fan (400°F/gas 6) and line two large baking trays (pans) with baking paper.

2   Next, make the frangipane by putting all the frangipane ingredients (except for the zest of 1 lemon) in a food processor and blitzing until smooth. (Or mix in a large mixing bowl with a wooden spoon using lots of elbow grease.)

3   Unroll the sheet of pastry on a clean work surface. Using a sharp knife, cut it into 12 small rectangles, measuring about 8 x 5 cm (3 x 2 in).

4   Spread a heaped teaspoon of frangipane in the centre of each pastry rectangle. Roll each pastry rectangle lengthways (see photo on page 72). Twist the rolled pastries slightly, as you would a cheese straw. Bring the two ends together to make a horseshoe shape and pinch them together. Transfer to the lined baking trays.

5   Using a pastry brush, dab the horseshoes with the extra tablespoon of milk. Sprinkle over the extra tablespoon of fennel seeds and bake for 35–40 minutes or until golden.

6   Using a sieve (strainer), dust the pastries with icing (confectioner's) sugar while still warm from the oven. Using a Microplane or fine side of a box grater, zest the remaining lemon over the pastries. Leave to cool.

7   The pastries will keep well for up to 2 days in an airtight container. Enjoy with a strong coffee.

Mid-morning

CAKE FOR COFFEE
PAGE 77

SOFT AMARETTI
PAGE 80

APPLE FRANGIPANE GALETTE
PAGE 82

LEMON EARL-GREY POLENTA LOAF
PAGE 84

YOGHURT CAKE
PAGE 89

SPINACH, DILL AND FETA FILO PIES
PAGE 90

THUMBPRINT COOKIES
PAGE 94

SEASONAL FRUIT FRIANDS
PAGE 96

Cake for Coffee

MAKES
8 slices (23-cm (9-in) cake)

TAKES
10 minutes, plus 35 minutes
baking time

Inspired by the beautifully simple breakfast cakes you find across Italy, for me, this is the perfect bake to enjoy with a strong espresso. The secret to the golden crumb is cold-pressed rapeseed oil or vibrant green light olive oil, but regular sunflower or vegetable oil gives a just as delicious result.

Also, how good is it that as an adult you can choose to eat cake for breakfast?!

150 ml (5 fl oz/scant ⅔ cup) light olive oil, rapeseed (canola) oil or sunflower oil, plus 1 teaspoon for greasing
250 g (9 oz/2 cups) plain (all-purpose) flour
250 g (9 oz/generous 1 cup) caster (superfine) sugar
3 teaspoons baking powder
150 g (5 oz) plain natural yoghurt
grated zest of 1 lemon
grated zest of ½ grapefruit or ½ orange
½ teaspoon vanilla paste
3 eggs
1½ tablespoons icing (confectioner's) sugar, for dusting

1   First, preheat the oven to 180°C fan (400°F/gas 6) and, using a pastry brush, grease a 23-cm (9-in) springform cake tin with oil.

2   Next, place the flour, sugar and baking powder in a large mixing bowl. Using a fork or balloon whisk, thoroughly mix together all the ingredients to ensure the baking powder is evenly distributed.

3   Next, throw in the yoghurt, oil, citrus zests and vanilla. Crack in the eggs and then stir until just combined.

4   Pour the batter into the greased tin and bake for 35 minutes, or until springy to the touch. While still warm, turn out the cake onto a large plate and, using a small sieve (strainer), dust with the icing sugar. Allow to cool for 10 minutes.

5   This cake keeps well for a couple of days when stored in an airtight container. Enjoy with thick, dark espresso.

Soft Amaretti

MAKES
8 amaretti

TAKES
25 minutes, plus 15 minutes
baking time

A crisp, golden crust with a squidgy, zesty, almondy centre, eating an amaretti with a strong coffee has got to be one of life's simplest pleasures. Considering how good they are, these amaretti are pretty easy to make, so I really urge you to give them a go.

1 egg white (save the egg yolk for the custard recipe on page 27)
100 g (3½ oz/scant ½ cup) caster (superfine) sugar
¾ teaspoon honey
½ teaspoon vanilla paste
finely grated zest of ¼ grapefruit, ⅓ orange or ½ lemon
150 g (5 oz/1½ cups) ground almonds
pinch of sea salt flakes
50 g (2 oz) icing (confectioner's) sugar

1   First, preheat the oven to 180°C fan (400°F/gas 6) and line a large baking tray (pan) with baking paper.

2   Next, place the egg white in a large bowl and beat until frothy using a handheld electric whisk or balloon whisk and plenty of elbow grease. Add the sugar and whisk for a further 2–3 minutes or until soft peaks have formed and the mixture is thick and glossy. Add the honey, vanilla paste and citrus zest and whisk for a further 30 seconds.

3   Using a large spoon or spatula, fold in the ground almonds and salt until just combined.

4   Spread the icing sugar over a large plate or tray. Don't bother sifting the sugar, just crush any large lumps between your fingers. Divide the amaretti mixture into 8 equal-sized balls. Roll the amaretti around in the icing sugar, packing as much sugar on the surface of each ball as possible. Leave the amaretti to sit in the sugar for 10 minutes.

5   Transfer the amaretti to the lined tray and bake for 15 minutes or until golden brown. Remove from the oven and leave to cool on the tray. The outsides will firm up but the insides of the amaretti will be all squidgy.

6   These amaretti keep beautifully in an airtight container for up to 3 days.

Apple Frangipane Galette

SERVES
6 (makes a 28-cm (11-in) tart)

TAKES
10 minutes to assemble (not including the pastry and frangipane preparation times), plus 50–55 minutes baking time

Although it looks rustic and homely, I can assure you this galette has the flavour of a sophisticated Parisian tart. I've made frangipane galettes with pretty much every fruit going and they never fail to please, so do experiment using whatever fruit you have to hand.

You really can't go wrong with a galette – the messier your presentation, the more inviting it will look. If this is your first time making a galette, just don't overwork the pastry and keep that butter nicely chilled and chunky. From that point on, you won't look back, I promise.

---

1 x quantity Basic Pastry (page 39), chilled in the fridge for at least 1 hour
plain (all-purpose) flour, for dusting
1 x quantity Basic Frangipane (page 45) made with almonds, at room temperature
3–4 large apples (either dessert or cooking apples work well), skin-on, core removed and thinly sliced
1 tablespoon milk, for brushing
sugar, for dusting (optional)

1   When the pastry has been chilling for 1 hour, preheat the oven to 180°C fan (400°F/gas 6).

2   Lay a sheet of baking paper on your work surface and lightly dust it with flour. Roll out the pastry to a rough circle, around 28 cm (11 in) in diameter, on the floured paper. You can use a rolling pin or even a wine bottle to do this and don't worry about the pastry circle being perfectly round or neat at the edges, in fact, the scruffier the shape, the better. Transfer the pastry circle – still on the paper – to the baking tray.

3   Using a spoon, carefully spread the frangipane over the pastry, leaving a 2-cm (¾-in) clear border all the way round. Cover the frangipane with the apple slices. Rather than arranging them in neat rows, I prefer the apples to be placed randomly and rustically, but you do as you wish.

4   Fold the edges of the pastry inwards to slightly overlap the fruit, pinching it slightly to create a crust. Brush the pastry crust with milk and bake in the preheated oven for 50–55 minutes or until golden and crisp. Remove from the oven and leave to cool slightly. To serve, sprinkle over some sugar, if using, then slice the galette into 6 (as you would a pizza).

5   This galette is best eaten on the day it's baked, but will still taste great the following day when left covered, but out of the fridge.

83   Mid-morning

Lemon Earl-Grey Polenta Loaf

MAKES
8 slices (900-g (2-lb) loaf cake)

TAKES
20 minutes, plus 45 minutes baking time

Bright and zingy in flavour and with a lovely grainy texture from the polenta, this loaf is optimism in cake form. Using rapeseed oil will give your cake an amazing sunny yellow colour. The Earl Grey adds an interesting citrus note of bergamot. If you can, try to use loose-leaf tea, but if that's out of reach, the contents of a few standard Earl Grey teabags work brilliantly, too.

---

250 ml (8½ fl oz/1 cup) cold-pressed rapeseed (canola) or vegetable oil
250 g (9 oz/generous 1 cup) caster (superfine) sugar, plus an extra 100 g (3½ oz/scant ½ cup) for the syrup
4 eggs
150 g (5 oz/1 cup) polenta
200 g (7 oz/1⅔ cups) plain (all-purpose) flour
2 teaspoons baking powder
3 teaspoons loose-leaf Earl Grey tea
grated zest and juice of 2 lemons (grate the zest on a Microplane or fine side of a box grater before juicing)

1 First, preheat the oven to 180°C fan (400°F/gas 6) and line a 900-g (2-lb) loaf tin (pan) with a strip of baking paper placed widthways.

2 Using a balloon whisk, combine the oil and sugar in a large bowl. Crack in the eggs, one a time, whisking between each addition.

3 In a separate bowl, combine the polenta, flour, baking powder and Earl Grey tea. Add the dry ingredients to the oil mixture, along with the lemon zest, and stir until just combined.

4 Scrape the batter into the lined tin and bake in the preheated oven for 45 minutes, or until risen and golden.

5 About 5 minutes before the cooking time is up, pour the lemon juice into a small pan and add the sugar for the syrup. Heat over a low–medium heat until you have a glossy syrup. Remove from the heat.

6 Once cooked, remove the cake from the oven. Using a skewer or tip of a sharp knife, gently poke 8 holes in the top of the cake while still in the tin and pour the syrup over. Leave to cool. Once cool, lift the cake out of the tin using the strip of baking paper and cut into slices.

7 Thanks to the lemon syrup, this loaf cake keeps well in an airtight container for up to 3–4 days.

Mid-morning

Yoghurt Cake

MAKES
8 large slices

TAKES
15 minutes, plus 45 minutes
baking time

This is a very simple sponge cake, which I always make when feeding a large crowd. If there are less people to serve, feel free to halve the quantities and use a smaller cake tin. You can also play around with the flavours, stirring a few handfuls of berries through the batter instead of the almonds before baking when you fancy something fruity.

300 g (10½ oz/1⅓ cup) caster (superfine) sugar
6 eggs
200 g (7 oz) strained natural yoghurt
200 ml (7 fl oz/scant 1 cup) olive or vegetable oil
450 g (1 lb/3½ cups) plain (all-purpose) flour
3 tablespoons baking powder
2 teaspoons vanilla paste
grated zest of 1 lemon
5 tablespoons flaked (slivered) almonds

1 First, preheat your oven to 180°C fan (400°F/gas 6) and line an 18 x 21-cm (7 x 8-in) tin (pan) with baking paper.

2 Using a wooden spoon in a large bowl, whisk the sugar and eggs until creamy. Add the yoghurt, oil, flour and baking powder and mix until smooth, then stir in the vanilla and lemon zest.

3 Scrape the mixture into the prepared tin, scatter the almonds over the top of the cake batter and bake in the preheated oven for 40–45 minutes or until golden and a skewer inserted into the middle of the cake comes out clean.

4 Leave to cool in the tin for 15 minutes and then turn out onto a wire rack to cool completely.

5 This cake is best eaten within one day of baking.

Spinach, Dill and Feta Filo Pies

After lemon, dill is my most-used savoury ingredient and here it mingles with bright greens, salty feta and crisp, flaky filo for a crowd-pleasing tray of golden hand pies. Serve up with a simple salad or some marinated tomatoes for a very pleasing snack.

MAKES
5 parcels

TAKES
35 minutes, plus 25 minutes baking time

250 g (9 oz) spinach, washed
60 g (2 oz) flat-leaf parsley
30 g (1 oz) dill
1 egg, beaten
200 g (7 oz) feta, crushed into small pieces
5 garlic cloves, peeled and crushed
grated zest of 1 lemon
⅛ teaspoon ground nutmeg
few turns of black pepper
35 g (1¼ oz) butter
15 sheets ready-rolled filo (phyllo) pastry (about 20 x 20 cm/8 x 8 in)

1   First, place the spinach, parsley and dill in a large pan, cover with water and bring to the boil. As soon as it reaches boiling, drain the spinach and herbs in a large colander. Once cool enough to handle, squeeze as much excess water from the greens as you can. Transfer to a cutting board, coarsely chop and then place in a large bowl.

2   Using a fork, stir in the beaten egg, feta, garlic, lemon zest, nutmeg and black pepper until nicely combined with the greens.

3   Preheat the oven to 180°C fan (400°F/gas 6) and line a large baking tray (pan) with baking paper.

4   Next, melt the butter in a small pan over a low heat. Lightly dampen a clean dish towel (this will be used to cover the filo sheets to prevent them from drying out). Remove the filo pastry sheets from their packaging. Place one sheet on your work surface and then cover the others with the damp dish towel.

5   Using a pastry brush, liberally brush the filo pastry sheet with melted butter. Place a second sheet on top and, again, liberally brush with butter. Layer on a third sheet and then spoon one-fifth of the greens mixture in the middle of the pastry.

6   Along one side, fold the edge of the pastry inwards over the greens, brushing lightly with butter to grease the 'seam'. Repeat this a further 4 times to create a rough pentagon shape. (While this may sound complicated, I promise you it's not.)

7   Place the parcel seam side down on the lined baking tray. Repeat with the remaining filo pastry sheets and greens mixture to create 5 parcels in total. Brush the tops of the parcels with any remaining butter and bake in the preheated oven for 25 minutes or until golden and crisp.

8   Serve warm with a punchy green salad or slices of ripe tomato dressed in plenty of good vinegar and sea salt. Or enjoy cold as a mid-morning snack or as part of a picnic.

Thumbprint Cookies

MAKES
18 small cookies

TAKES
10 minutes, plus 12 minutes
baking time

This is a beautifully plain, crumbly cookie, making it the ideal blank canvas for adding chopped herbs, such as tarragon, rosemary, or thyme, or citrus zest, such as lemon or grapefruit. If you've got an interesting jam to play with, you can just leave the cookie dough as it is without adding any optional extras. Try using one of the jam flavours on page 33, or one of your own creations, perhaps?

125 g (4 oz) butter (salted
   or unsalted), soft/at room
   temperature
100 g (3½ oz/scant ½ cup) caster
   (superfine) sugar
1 egg
2 teaspoons vanilla paste
300 g (10½ oz/2½ cups) plain
   (all-purpose) flour
40 g (1½ oz/generous ⅓ cup)
   ground almonds
½ teaspoon baking powder
pinch of sea salt flakes

Optional extras
1–2 tablespoons finely chopped
   tarragon or other herb
   of your choice
9 teaspoons of your favourite jam

1   First, preheat the oven to 180°C fan (400°F/gas 6) and line a baking tray (pan) with baking paper.

2   Using a handheld electric whisk, beat the butter, sugar, egg and vanilla paste together in a large bowl. If the mixture curdles, don't worry, just whisk in 1 tablespoon of the flour.

3   Next, stir in the flour, almonds, baking powder, salt and chopped herbs, if using, until you have a rough, crumbly, soft dough. Transfer to a work surface and knead until smooth.

4   Roll the dough into 18 equal-sized balls (roughly 30 g/1 oz each) and place them on the lined baking tray, leaving space between each one to allow for spreading. Press your thumb into the middle of each cookie to create a little indent.

5   Fill each indent with ½ teaspoon jam (if using) and bake in the preheated oven for 12 minutes or until golden. Remove from the oven and leave to cool on the tray, where they'll continue to firm up nicely.

6   These cookies keep well overnight in an airtight container.

Seasonal Fruit Friands

Made from nutty brown butter, ground almonds and frothy egg whites, these light, dainty cakes are so easy, yet so good. Use this recipe as a blank canvas and top them with whatever fruit is in season and best at any moment. And good luck eating only one at a time!

MAKES
10 friands

TAKES
20 minutes, plus 15–20 minutes baking time

180 g (6½ oz) butter (salted or unsalted)
50 g (2 oz/generous ⅓ cup) plain (all-purpose) flour
180 g (6½ oz/1½ cups) icing (confectioner's) sugar
100 g (3½ oz/1 cup) ground almonds
grated zest of 2 lemons (save the lemon juice for the jam recipes on page 33)
5 egg whites (save the egg yolks for the custard recipe on page 27)
pinch of sea salt flakes

<u>Optional fruit fillings</u>
20–30 blackberries
20–30 x 2-cm (¾-in) rhubarb pieces
20–30 x 2-cm (¾-in) apple, pear or plum chunks

1   First, preheat the oven to 180°C fan (400°F/gas 6).

2   Next, melt the butter in a small saucepan over a medium-high heat and warm it for 5–7 minutes or until it becomes a dark, nutty, golden colour, although do not to take it too far and completely burn it. Remove from the heat and leave to cool slightly. Using a pastry brush, grease 10 of the moulds in a cupcake baking tray (pan) or friand tray, if you have one, with some of the melted butter.

3   Meanwhile, combine the flour and icing sugar in a large mixing bowl. (If the sugar is lumpy, sift it first.) Stir in the ground almonds and lemon zest.

4   In a separate large bowl and using a balloon whisk, beat the egg whites to a soft, light foam. Add the whisked egg whites to the flour mixture along with the melted butter. Gently fold everything together with a metal spoon until lightly but thoroughly combined.

5   Spoon the batter evenly into the buttered moulds. Pop 2 or 3 pieces of your chosen fruit in the centre of each mould and bake in the preheated oven for 15–20 minutes or until risen, golden and springy to the touch. Remove from the oven and leave the friands to settle for 20 minutes before carefully removing them from the moulds using a knife.

6   These friands are really moist so they keep well in an airtight container for up to 3 days.

Mid-morning

Lunch

PORK AND FENNEL SAUSAGE ROLLS
PAGE 102

TOMATO, PARMESAN AND CAPER GALETTES
PAGE 104

SAGE, GARLIC AND CHEESE LOAF FOR SOUP
PAGE 108

CHEDDAR AND MUSTARD SCONES
PAGE 109

CHICKEN CURRY PIE
PAGE 112

JAM AND COCONUT SPONGE
PAGE 115

ELLIOTT'S SEA SALT CHOCOLATE COOKIES
PAGE 116

MARMITE BROWNIES
PAGE 121

Pork and Fennel Sausage Rolls

Every single day at Elliott's, within the first few hours of opening, we sell out of these sausage rolls. So I've got a very good feeling you're going to enjoy making them in your own home, too!

It's the generous use of herbs and spices that really makes these sausage rolls special, so have a play with throwing in other combinations you think up, too.

MAKES
8 sausage rolls

TAKES
30 minutes, plus 50 minutes–1 hour baking time

---

3 teaspoons fennel seeds, lightly crushed, plus extra for sprinkling
large bunch of flat-leaf parsley, finely chopped, including stalks (around 25 g/1 oz)
5 spring onions (scallions), finely chopped
4 garlic cloves, peeled and crushed
1 teaspoon sea salt flakes or ½ teaspoon fine salt
good grinding of black pepper
6 pork sausages (about 400 g/14 oz)
1 sheet ready-rolled all-butter puff pastry (about 375 g/13 oz)
1 egg

1 First, preheat the oven to 180°C fan (400°F/gas 6) and line 2 baking trays (pans) with baking paper.

2 Next, put the fennel seeds, parsley, spring onions, garlic, salt and pepper in a large mixing bowl. Cut the sausages from their skins (the skins can be discarded) then, using your hands, mix until really well combined with the parsley mixture.

3 Wash your hands then unroll the pastry sheet. Halve the pastry lengthways with a sharp knife to give you 2 long rectangles. Place each rectangle on the lined baking tray. Halve the sausage mixture then place it in a long line down the middle of each rectangle. (You want the sausage to sit right up to the end of the pastry as it'll shrink in the oven slightly when cooking.)

4 Beat the egg in a small bowl with a fork then, using your fingers or a pastry brush, paint one side of each rectangle with the egg. Fold the pastry over to create a little blanket roll then, using a fork, crimp the edge to give the rolls a nice pattern. Brush the top of each roll with the remaining egg then sprinkle over a few extra fennel seeds. Cut each roll into 4 to give you 8 sausage rolls in total.

5 Bake for 50 minutes–1 hour or until really deep golden. Allow to cool for 10 minutes before eating them warm on their own, or with a lemony dressed salad, or leave to cool completely.

6 They will keep in an airtight container for another day before the pastry turns a bit soggy.

Tomato, Parmesan and Caper Galettes

SERVES
4

TAKES
15 minutes, plus 15–20 minutes
baking time

Once you've mastered the basics of making flaky, buttery galette pastry (check out my top tips on page 40), the possibilities for creating delicious meals in rustic, open pie form are endless.

Here, I've thrown on tomatoes, parmesan and capers as I tend to always have those in the fridge, but play about with whatever you have to hand. A galette really is the tastiest canvas for other simple ingredients.

---

1 x quantity Basic Pastry (page 39),
    chilled in the fridge for at least
    1 hour
plain flour for dusting
40 g (1½) Parmesan
250 g (9 oz) cherry tomatoes, halved
2 tablespoons capers
1 tablespoon milk
2 stalks tarragon (optional)

---

1   When the pastry has been chilling for 1 hour, preheat the oven to 180°C fan (400°F/gas 6).

2   Lay a sheet of baking paper on your work surface and lightly dust it with flour. Divide the pastry into 4 then rollout to create 4 rough circles, around 11 cm (4 in) in diameter each, on the floured paper. You can use a rolling pin or even a wine bottle to do this and don't worry about the pastry circles being perfectly round or neat at the edges; in fact, the scruffier the shapes, the better. Transfer the pastry circles – still on the paper – to the baking tray.

3   Using a microplane or fine side of a box grater, grate the Parmesan over the base of each pastry. Then top with the tomatoes and capers, leaving a 1 cm (½ in) border around the edge of each.

4   Fold the edges of the pastry inwards to overlap the filling, pinching it slightly to create a crust. Using a pastry brush, dab the crust with milk and bake in the preheated oven for 35 minutes, or until golden and crisp at the edges. Remove from the oven and leave to cool slightly.

5   Serve up with lemony-dressed salad then pick over the tarragon leaves if using.

6   The galettes are best eaten fresh, but will keep for another day when left covered, but out of the fridge. You can reheat them or enjoy at room temperature.

Sage, Garlic and Cheese Loaf for Soup

Think giant cheese scone meets garlic bread in this comforting loaf. It's a doddle to whip up – you probably have most of the ingredients in the house already – and it will definitely make a bowl of soup extra special. You can use half the quantity of cheese that I have specified below, but I like to load this loaf up with cheese!

SERVES
6

TAKES
20 minutes, plus 25–30 minutes baking time

350 g (12 oz/2¾ cups) plain (all-purpose) flour, plus extra for dusting
4 tablespoons cold-pressed rapeseed (canola) oil or olive oil
15 g (½ oz) sage, leaves picked and coarsely chopped
4 garlic cloves, peeled and thinly sliced
1 teaspoon sea salt flakes, plus extra for sprinkling
1 teaspoon baking powder
85 g (3 oz) butter, ideally cold, cut into cubes
200 g (7 oz) strained natural yoghurt
125 g (4 oz) hard cheese, like Cheddar or Gruyère, grated or finely chopped

1 First, preheat the oven to 220°C fan (475°F/gas 9) and dust a large baking tray (pan) with flour.

2 Next, heat the oil in a small frying pan (skillet) over a high heat, add the sage and garlic and fry for 2–3 minutes or until golden and crisp (take care not to burn them). Carefully transfer to a bowl where the garlic will continue to cook in the hot oil.

3 Place the flour, salt, baking powder and butter in a food processor, then pulse until there are no more big chunks of butter visible. (Or you can do this using your hands by rubbing the ingredients between your fingers in a large bowl until you get chunky breadcrumbs).

4 Transfer the mixture to your work surface. Create a little well in the middle, spoon the yoghurt into the well and then, using your hands, gently knead until you have a scruffy dough. Tip in the sage and garlic, along with any oil, as well as the cheese. Knead a few more times until combined then shape into a round loaf, about 15 cm (6 in) wide.

5 Transfer the loaf to the floured tray, sprinkle with sea salt and then bake in the preheated oven for 25–30 minutes or until golden.

6 This loaf is best eaten on the day it is baked, ideally warm from the oven and with a comforting bowl of soup.

Cheddar and Mustard Scones

These are rainy day comfort food, generous with cheese, a hint of mustard bringing a subtle tang, and ready in under 25 minutes. For the flakiest scones with a great rise, don't be tempted to knead as you'll overwork the dough. A lazy, scruffy approach definitely gives the most delicious results here – my kind of baking!

MAKES
6 scones

TAKE
10 minutes, plus 15 minutes baking time

---

225 g (8 oz) self-raising flour, plus extra for dusting
1 teaspoon baking powder
¾ teaspoon sea salt flakes
55 g (2 oz) cold salted or unsalted butter, cut into cubes
1 teaspoon Dijon mustard, or ½ teaspoon English mustard, (optional)
120 ml (4 fl oz/½ cup) milk, ideally whole, but any will do
150 g (5 oz) mature Cheddar, finely grated

1. First, preheat the oven to 220°C fan (475°F/gas 9) and place a large baking sheet in there to preheat (this will give your scones a lovely, crisp bottom).

2. In a large bowl, whisk the flour, baking powder and salt together until well combined.

3. Next, add the butter and mustard (if using) then, using your index and middle fingers and thumbs, rub until you've got large, rough flakes. (Don't worry if some of the butter remains quite chunky.) Work in the milk and 100 g (3½ oz) of the cheese until just combined to a scruffy dough, then turn out onto your worktop, lighted dusted with flour.

4. Using your hands, press into a large rectangle around 2.5 cm (1 in) thick. Don't be tempted to knead it! Cut into 6 large scones, push in the square edges to round them slightly, then transfer to the hot tray.

5. Sprinkle over the remaining 50 g (2 oz) cheese and bake for 15 minutes or until golden brown and cooked in the middle (you can test by cutting one open and checking it's not too doughy).

6. The scones are best eaten on the day they're made, but can be toasted the next day and spread with lots of extra butter! (Make sure you eat the crispy cheese from the baking tray; it tastes like the edges of a good cheese toastie!)

Chicken Curry Pie

MAKES
enough for 4 people

TAKES
25 minutes, plus 50 minutes baking time, plus time to make the pastry ahead

This is what I think of as match-day pie, as it's the snack I would always eat at half time with my dad in the stadium watching Sunderland play football. The pastry is the one from the Baking Basics chapter (page 39) and the filling is a hack way of quickly creating the flavour of a chicken curry. Of course, you can always throw in your other favourite fillings too!

1 x quantity Basic Pastry (page 39), chilled
plain (all-purpose) flour, for dusting
1 egg yolk, for brushing
wilted greens, to serve

Chicken curry filling
3 tablespoons rapeseed/vegetable oil
2 small onions, finely sliced
650 g (1 lb 7 oz) chicken thighs, skinless, boneless, roughly chopped
4 garlic cloves, peeled and crushed
1 teaspoon sea salt flakes
2 tablespoons curry power
1 teaspoon ground cumin
1 teaspoon garam masala
1 tablespoon tomato purée (paste)
½ teaspoon dried chilli flakes (hot red pepper flakes)
5 tablespoons natural strained yoghurt
2 tomatoes, finely chopped

1   First, preheat the oven to 180°C fan (400°F/gas 6).

2   Next, make the filling. Heat 2 tablespoons of the oil in a large pan over medium-high heat. Once hot, add the onions and fry for 4 minutes or until beginning to soften. Increase the heat to high, add the remaining 1 tablespoon oil and the chicken thighs to the pan and fry for a further 6 minutes to seal and lightly brown the meat.

3   Reduce the heat to low, stir in the garlic, salt and spices, then fry for 2 minutes or until fragrant. Stir in the tomato purée, dried chilli flakes, yoghurt and tomatoes. Remove from the heat and set aside.

4   Lightly dust your work surface and rolling pin with flour. Roll out two-thirds of the pastry to fit a medium-sized baking dish. The dish I use is 26 x 19 x 6 cm (10 x 7½ x 2 in).

5   Using a fork, prick the base of the pastry case a few times, then cover with a sheet of baking paper. Cover the base of the dish with baking beans or rice to weigh the pastry down and bake in the preheated oven for 20 minutes.

6   After 20 minutes, remove the baking beans or rice (if using rice, don't discard as it can be used time and time again) and baking paper. Fill the pastry case with the chicken curry filling.

7   Roll out the remaining pastry to make the pie lid and lay it over the top of the filling. Cut out any decoration you like from the pastry offcuts and add it to the pie lid (I like to keep it simple and just use the word 'pie'). Using a fork, press all the way round the pie lid to crimp and seal the edges, then brush with egg yolk. Return to the oven and bake for a further 30 minutes or until golden and crisp.

8   Serve the pie while piping hot, perhaps with some wilted greens on the side.

9   This pie is best eaten on the day of baking, although slightly soggy pastry leftovers are delicious the next day, too!

Jam and Coconut Sponge

MAKES
8 slices

TAKES
15 minutes, plus 30 minutes
baking time

Our customers always smile whenever they see this cake on the Elliott's counter, as it reminds them of the warm sponge pudding served during school dinners when they were children. Here I've used a jar of quick Blueberry and Rosemary Jam from the Baking Basics chapter (page 33), but of course you can swap in your favourite shop-bought jam, if you prefer.

225 g (8 oz) butter, at room temperature, plus extra for greasing
225 g (8 oz/1 cup) caster (superfine) sugar
4 large eggs
225 g (8 oz/1¾ cups) self-raising flour
½ teaspoon baking powder
1 x quantity Blueberry and Rosemary Jam (page 33), or any jar of shop-bought jam
75 g (2½ oz) desiccated (shredded) coconut
1 x quantity of Proper Traditional Custard (page 27), to serve

1   First, preheat the oven to 180°C fan (400°F/gas 6) and grease the bottom of a 28 x 22-cm (11 x 8.5-in) baking tin (pan), then line it with baking paper.

2   Using a wooden spoon in a large mixing bowl, cream together the butter and sugar until pale and fluffy. Crack in the eggs, one at a time, beating between each addition.

3   Next, fold in the flour and baking powder, making sure the baking powder is well incorporated.

4   Scrape the batter into the lined tin and bake in the preheated oven for 25–30 minutes or until golden.

5   Remove the tray from the oven and spread the jam over the top of the warm sponge, then evenly scatter over the coconut. Slice the sponge cake into portions and enjoy warm with custard. It can also be eaten cold when allowed to cool in the tin.

6   This sponge cake is best eaten within a day of baking.

Elliott's Sea Salt Chocolate Cookies

Defining what makes the perfect cookie is, of course, a very personal thing. For me though, this is the one. It has a crisp edge, a squidgy centre and enough flaky sea salt to balance the sugar and chocolate.

MAKES
10 cookies

TAKES
20 minutes, plus 14 minutes
baking time

110 g (3¾ oz) butter (salted
or unsalted), soft/at room
temperature, cut into rough cubes
160 g (5½ oz/scant 1 cup) soft light
brown sugar
50 g (2 oz/¼ cup) caster
(superfine) sugar
1 egg
½ teaspoon vanilla paste
200 g (7 oz/1⅔ cups) plain
(all-purpose) flour
½ teaspoon baking powder
½ teaspoon bicarbonate of soda
(baking soda)
½ teaspoon fine salt
150 g (5 oz) good-quality dark
(bittersweet) chocolate, chopped
1 teaspoon sea salt flakes

1   Preheat the oven to 180°C fan (400°F/gas 6) and line 2 large baking trays (baking pans) with baking paper.

2   Next, using an electric handheld whisk in a large bowl, beat the butter until it's really soft. Add the sugars and beat for a further 2 minutes, then add the egg and vanilla and beat until combined. (You can also use a wooden spoon and lots of elbow grease to do all the above.)

3   In a separate large mixing bowl, combine the flour, baking powder, bicarbonate of soda and fine salt. Using a fork or balloon whisk, thoroughly mix together all the ingredients to ensure the bicarbonate of soda is evenly distributed.

4   Tip the dry ingredients into the butter mixture along with the chocolate, then stir with a wooden spoon until combined. Using your hands, push together any bits that are sitting in the bottom of the bowl until you have a dough.

5   Roll the dough into 10 equal-sized balls and place them on the lined baking trays, leaving space between each one to allow for spreading. Bake in the preheated oven for 14 minutes. After this time, the cookies may look slightly under-baked, but they will crisp up at the edges as they cool. Remove from the oven and sprinkle the cookies with the sea salt flakes and allow to cool.

6   These cookies keep well in an airtight container for up to 4 days.

TIP

You can also make and freeze the dough ahead, then bake the dough balls in smaller batches – just add an extra 4 minutes to the baking time when baking from frozen.

Tahini works really well with these cookies, just beat 2 tablespoons tahini into the butter before adding the sugar. You can also sprinkle with white or black sesame seeds too.

Marmite Brownies

MAKES
16 brownies

TAKES
20 minutes, plus 25 minutes
baking time

The inclusion of Marmite in a brownie may sound slightly odd, but trust me on this. The salty yeast spread naturally seasons the chocolate in the cake mixture, meaning it tastes even richer and fudgier. Of course, you can just use a generous pinch of sea salt if you don't have any Marmite (or Vegemite, if you're from the Southern Hemisphere) in the house.

200 g (7 oz) good-quality dark (bittersweet) chocolate, roughly chopped
150 g (5 oz) unsalted butter
1 tablespoon Marmite (yeast extract) or Vegemite
3 eggs
250 g (9 oz/generous 1 cup) caster (superfine) sugar
50 g (2 oz/generous ⅓ cup) plain (all-purpose) flour
80 g (3 oz) almonds or hazelnuts (either skin-on or blanched)

1   First, preheat the oven to 160°C fan (350°F/gas 4) and line a 23-cm (9-in) square baking tin (pan) with baking paper.

2   Next, gently melt the chocolate, butter and Marmite together in a large bowl set above a pan of gently simmering water, ensuring the water doesn't touch the base of the bowl. Once melted and melded together, set aside to cool slightly.

3   Using a balloon whisk in a separate large mixing bowl, beat the eggs and sugar. Gently ladle in a few spoonfuls of the melted chocolate mixture, whisking continuously to ensure the batter doesn't split.

4   Pour in the remaining chocolate mixture, while whisking continuously – if you continue to whisk, your batter won't split but will thicken beautifully. If it does split, don't panic – simply blitz with a stick (immersion) blender for a few seconds to bring everything back together.

5   Using a spatula or wooden spoon, gently fold in the flour and almonds or hazelnuts until just combined.

6   Scrape the batter into the lined tin and bake in the preheated oven for 20–25 minutes or until a lovely crust forms on top of the brownie. Allow to cool completely in the tin before cutting into slices.

7   These brownies keep well in an airtight container for up to 3 days.

Afternoon

GRAPEFRUIT DRIZZLE LOAF
PAGE 124

ONE-JAR PEANUT BUTTER COOKIES
PAGE 126

MY GO-TO BROWN SUGAR SPONGE
PAGE 128

STICKY TRIPLE GINGER CAKE
PAGE 131

SUGAR BUNS FOR TEA
PAGE 132

OLIVE OIL, CHOCOLATE
AND ORANGE LOAF
PAGE 134

NO-CHURN CRÈME
FRAÎCHE ICE CREAM
PAGE 136

CHOCOLATE TRUFFLES
FOR PHILLIPPA
PAGE 139

Grapefruit Drizzle Loaf

MAKES
8 slices (900-g (2-lb) loaf cake)

TAKES
10 minutes, plus 40 minutes
baking time

Grapefruit brings a sunny, tang to this light and fluffy loaf cake, but of course you can use lemon, lime or orange if that's what you've got to hand. I recommend using a handheld electric whisk to throw the batter together quickly, but a wooden spoon and plenty of elbow grease gives brilliant results, too. If making by hand, just cream the butter and sugar together first, before adding the eggs.

---

175 g (6 oz/⅔ cup) caster (superfine) sugar
175 g (6 oz/1⅓ cups) self-raising flour
¾ teaspoon baking powder
175 g (6 oz) butter (salted or unsalted), soft/at room temperature, plus extra for greasing
3 eggs
grated zest of ½ grapefruit (grate the zest on a Microplane or fine side of a box grater before juicing)
juice of 1 grapefruit
100 g (3½ oz/scant ½ cup) granulated white sugar

1   First, preheat the oven to 180°C fan (400°F/gas 6) and line a 900-g (2-lb) loaf tin (pan) with a strip of baking paper placed widthways.

2   Using a handheld electric whisk, beat together the caster (superfine) sugar, flour, baking powder, butter, eggs and grapefruit zest until smooth in a large mixing bowl.

3   Scrape the batter into the lined tin and bake in the preheated oven for 40 minutes, or until risen and golden brown. Remove the cake from the oven and leave to cool slightly.

4   Meanwhile, stir together the grapefruit juice and granulated white sugar in a small bowl for the syrup.

5   While the sponge is still warm, using a skewer or tip of a sharp knife, gently poke 8 holes in the top of the cake while still in the tin and pour the syrup over. Leave to cool. Once cool, lift the cake out of the tin using the strip of baking paper and cut into slices.

6   Thanks to the grapefruit drizzle, this loaf cake keeps well in an airtight container for up to 2 days.

One-Jar Peanut Butter Cookies

MAKES
12 cookies

TAKES
10 minutes, plus 12 minutes baking time

Sometimes you just *need* to fix that craving for a little sweet treat and these cookies never fail to deliver. You can easily memorise this recipe as it's only four ingredients: peanut butter, sugar, an egg and a pinch of salt. They're that simple and ready for you to enjoy in less than 25 minutes.

Here, I've pressed a whole star anise into the top of each cookie to imprint its shape, but you can lightly press the cookies with the tines of a fork, if that's easier for you. The chocolate version tastes very similar to a certain brand of peanut butter cup, while the jam version, well... jam and peanut butter is a classic combination that simply can't be messed with.

---

1 x 225 g (8 oz) jar of good-quality peanut butter (crunchy or smooth, ideally 100 per cent peanuts with no palm oil or other additives)
heavy pinch of sea salt flakes
¾ jar caster (superfine) sugar
1 egg

1   First, preheat the oven to 180°C fan (400°F/gas 6) and line a baking tray (pan) with baking paper.

2   Using a wooden spoon, stir together all the ingredients in a large mixing bowl to make a smooth paste. Once the dough comes together it will suddenly transform into a dry texture – that's when you know it's ready to roll out.

3   Roll the dough into 12 walnut-sized balls and transfer to the lined baking tray, leaving space between each one to allow the for spreading. Bake for 12 minutes in the preheated oven. Leave to cool for a couple of minutes before eating.

4   These cookies keep well in an airtight container for a couple of days... but good luck with that!

PEANUT BUTTER AND JAM COOKIES

6 teaspoons jam in any flavour that you prefer

1   Using a teaspoon, make a small well in each ball of dough and then fill the space with ½ teaspoon jam before baking.

PEANUT BUTTER AND CHOCOLATE COOKIES

75 g (2½ oz) good-quality dark (bittersweet) chocolate

1   Break the chocolate into 12 small chunks and then press a piece into each ball of dough before baking.

My Go-To Brown Sugar Sponge (with seasonal fruit)

Think of this recipe as a reliable friend in your kitchen; always there to support whichever fruit is sitting in your fruit bowl, no matter the time of year.

The ground almonds in the sponge result in a lovely squidgy crumb, so you definitely don't need to worry about it turning out dry. Life's far too short for dry cake! The brown sugar lends a caramel-like quality to the cake, but you can use any white sugar if that's all you have – the cake will still be delicious.

MAKES
8 slices (23-cm (9-in) cake)

TAKES
20 minutes, plus 1 hour baking time

---

175 g (6 oz) butter (salted or unsalted), soft/at room temperature, plus 1 tablespoon for greasing
150 g (5 oz/generous ¾ cup) soft dark brown sugar
2 eggs
1 teaspoon vanilla paste
125 g (4 oz/1¼ cup) ground almonds
175 g (6 oz/1⅓ cups) plain (all-purpose) flour
2 teaspoons baking powder
¼ teaspoon sea salt flakes

Optional fruit toppings
250 g (9 oz) fruit, such as:
- blood oranges, sliced
- rhubarb stalks, cut into 2-cm (¾-in) pieces
- apples, cored and sliced
- strawberries, hulled and halved
- gooseberries, halved
- cherries, stoned (pitted)

1   First, preheat the oven to 160°C fan (350°F/gas 4) and use the extra tablespoon of butter to grease a 23-cm (9-in) springform cake tin (pan) then line the base and sides with baking paper.

2   Using a handheld electric whisk, beat together the butter, sugar, eggs and vanilla in a large mixing bowl until smooth and fluffy. (Or beat the ingredients together with a wooden spoon in a large bowl with plenty of elbow grease.)

3   In a separate large mixing bowl, combine the almonds, flour, baking powder and salt. Using a fork or balloon whisk, thoroughly mix together all the ingredients to ensure the baking powder is evenly distributed.

4   Fold the dry ingredients into the butter mixture until just combined. You may feel it's quite a dry batter for a sponge cake, but I promise you that it will be delicious!

5   Scrape the batter into the lined tin and top with your chosen fruit. Bake in the preheated for 1 hour or until risen and springy to the touch – a skewer or knife inserted into the middle of the cake should come out clean. Remove from the oven and leave to cool in the tin. After 20 minutes, lift the cake out of the tin and cut into slices.

6   This cake keeps well in an airtight container for up to 3 days.

Sticky Triple Ginger Cake

MAKES
8 slices (23-cm (9-in) cake)

TAKES
35 minutes, plus 1 hour baking time

Picking a favourite recipe in a book is always tricky (a bit like picking a favourite child!), but for me it's got to be this one. With three types of ginger – ground, fresh and stem – this cake is sticky, spiced and contains just the right amount of sweetness from the treacle.

The best part is that this cake tastes even better with time. Try a slice on day three, if you can get it to last that long! It's just incredible with an afternoon cuppa, or later in the evening with a big jug of custard or even a wedge of mature Cheddar cheese.

125 ml (4¼ fl oz/½ cup) vegetable, light olive or rapeseed (canola) oil, plus 1 tablespoon for greasing
225 g (8 oz/1¼ cups) soft dark brown sugar
85 g (3 oz) black treacle (blackstrap molasses)
150 g (5 oz) golden syrup
1½ tablespoons ground ginger
¼ teaspoon ground cloves
1 teaspoon ground cinnamon
1 teaspoon garam masala
20 g (¾ oz) fresh ginger
3 pieces of preserved stem ginger in syrup
1 egg
300 g (10½ oz/2½ cups) self-raising flour
½ teaspoon baking powder
350 ml (12 fl oz/1½ cups) milk (ideally whole/full-fat)
1 x quantity of Proper Traditional Custard (page 27), to serve

1   First, preheat the oven to 160°C fan (350°F/gas 4). Using a pastry brush or a piece of kitchen paper, lightly grease a 23-cm (9-in) springform cake tin (pan), then line the base and sides with baking paper.

2   Next, gently heat the oil, sugar, black treacle, golden syrup and spices in a large saucepan over a low heat. Stir occasionally with a wooden spoon until all the sugar has dissolved, then remove from the heat once smooth and set aside to cool. (You may suspect that I've confused the quantities of oil and syrup, but I promise you they're right and will mix together.)

3   While the oil mixture is cooling, finely grate in the fresh ginger (there's no need to peel it) into the pan, finely chop the stem ginger and add that, too, then stir to combine. By this point, the mixture should be cool enough for you to comfortably dip your finger in. If not, leave it to cool for a few more minutes.

4   Crack in the egg and then stir to combine (as you've allowed the mixture to cool, it won't scramble). Stir in one-quarter of the flour, along with the baking powder. Continue to stir in the remaining flour and then mix thoroughly until smooth. Stir in one direction only in order to prevent any lumps forming by a change in direction.

5   Next, splash in one-quarter of the milk to loosen the batter. Stir in the remaining milk until combined – it might look too thin, or like it's not coming together, but keep stirring until smooth.

6   Scrape the batter into the lined tin and bake in the preheated oven for 1 hour, or until firm to the touch. Remove the tin from the oven and leave the cake to cool slightly. Slice the cake into portions and enjoy warm with custard. It can also be eaten cold when allowed to cool in the tin.

7   This cake keeps well in an airtight container for up to 5 days. In fact, it tastes even better after a couple of days and is incredible eaten with strong cheeses, such as a mature Cheddar.

Sugar Buns for Tea

MAKES
12 buns

TAKES
10 minutes, plus 25 minutes baking time and 25 minutes cooling time

These buns are incredibly light and fluffy, somewhere between a cupcake and the inside of a cinnamon doughnut. They are best when teamed up with a pot of strong tea.

The garam masala isn't a must, I just always have it in the cupboard for making curries with. If there's none in your cupboard, don't worry; stick with the cinnamon, or improvise with some ground cardamom or ground ginger instead.

---

85 ml (2¾ fl oz/⅓ cup) cold-pressed rapeseed (canola) oil, plus extra for greasing
225 g (8 oz/1¾ cups) plain (all-purpose) flour
100 g (3½ oz/scant ½ cup) caster (superfine) sugar, plus 150 g (5 oz/ generous ⅔ cup) extra for dipping
2½ teaspoons baking powder
1 teaspoon ground cinnamon, plus ½ teaspoon for dipping
¾ teaspoon garam masala, plus ¼ teaspoon for dipping
pinch of sea salt flakes, plus an extra small pinch for dipping
1 egg
225 ml (8 fl oz/scant 1 cup) milk (ideally whole/full-fat, but any will do)

1   First, preheat the oven to 180°C fan (400°F/gas 6). Using a pastry brush, liberally grease a 12-hole muffin tin (tray), making sure you the base and sides of each hole are well oiled.

2   Next, place all the remaining ingredients (except the extra sugar, cinnamon, garam masala and salt for dipping) in a large mixing bowl. Using a balloon whisk, beat everything together until just combined – don't worry if there are a few lumps in the batter. (Don't be tempted to use a handheld electric whisk for this as it'll ruin the fluffy texture.)

3   Spoon the batter into the 12 holes of the muffin tin. If it makes life easier, transfer the batter to a jug (pitcher) and then pour the batter into the holes with fewer drips! Bake in the preheated oven for 25 minutes, or until golden and springy to touch.

4   Remove the tin from the oven and, taking care not to burn yourself, run a knife around the outside edge of each bun – this makes it easier to get them out of the tin once cool. Leave to cool in the tin for 25 minutes.

5   Meanwhile, combine the extra sugar, cinnamon, garam masala and salt in a small shallow bowl. Carefully remove the buns from the tin and then roll them in the spiced sugar.

6   These are best eaten within a day of baking.

Afternoon

Olive Oil, Chocolate and Orange Loaf

Here, I've teamed the classic pairing of chocolate and orange with the grassy fragrance of olive oil for a crowd-pleasing loaf cake. If you don't have enough olive oil in stock, you can use cold-pressed rapeseed (canola) oil or regular vegetable oil instead – the cake will be just as delicious!

MAKES
8 slices (900-g (2-lb) loaf)

TAKES
15 minutes, plus 40 minutes
baking time

250 ml (8½ fl oz/1 cup) olive oil,
    cold-pressed rapeseed (canola) oil
    or vegetable oil, plus extra
    for greasing
150 ml (5 fl oz/scant ⅔ cup) milk
    (ideally whole/full-fat)
3 eggs
300 g (10½ oz/2½ cups) plain
    (all-purpose) flour
125 g (4½ oz/½ cup) caster
    (superfine) sugar
1½ teaspoon baking powder
¼ teaspoon fine salt
100 g (3½ oz) dark (bittersweet)
    chocolate, minimum 60% cocoa
    solids, finely chopped
grated zest of 1 orange
2 tablespoons demerara
    (turbinado) sugar

1   First, preheat the oven to 180°C fan (400°F/gas 6) and grease and line a 900-g (2-lb) loaf tin (pan) with a strip of baking paper placed widthways.

2   Using a balloon whisk, beat together the oil, milk and eggs in a large mixing bowl.

3   In a separate large mixing bowl, combine the flour, caster sugar, baking powder and salt. Using a balloon whisk, thoroughly mix together all the ingredients to ensure the baking powder is evenly distributed.

4   Gradually add the oil mixture to the dry ingredients, but taking care not to overwork the batter. Fold in the chopped chocolate and orange zest.

5   Scrape the batter into the lined tin and sprinkle over the demerara sugar. Bake in the preheated oven for 40 minutes, or until golden brown – a skewer or knife inserted into the middle of the cake should come out clean. Remove from the oven and leave to cool in the tin. Once cool, lift the cake out of the tin using the strip of baking paper and cut into slices.

6   Thanks to the oil, this cake keeps well in an airtight container for up to 3 days.

No-Churn Crème Fraîche Ice Cream

MAKES
5–6 scoops

TAKES
5 minutes

The instructions for making this ice cream are already given in the custard section of Baking Basics at the front of this book (page 27), but I just had to feature it in its own right. It's been such a game changer in our house – only 5 minutes to prepare, no churning required and definitely no need for a specialist ice-cream maker.

There's brightness from the lemon, comforting familiarity from the vanilla, and a clean, sophisticated tartness from the crème fraîche. Just make sure you buy full-fat crème fraîche as an afternoon treat in the sun is not the moment for scrimping on good dairy. Please join me in making this ice cream, it really is a dream.

---

300 g (10½ oz) crème fraîche (ideally full-fat)
6 tablespoons caster (superfine) sugar
1 teaspoon vanilla paste
pinch of sea salt flakes
3 egg yolks (save the egg whites for the Soft Amaretti on page 80 or Hazelnut and Brown Sugar Pavlova on page 156)
grated zest of 1 lemon (optional)

1   Place all the ingredients in a medium saucepan then, using a balloon whisk, beat until completely smooth.

2   Place over the lowest heat and, stirring regularly, heat the mixture until warm, ensuring it doesn't catch on the base of the pan.

3   Transfer the mixture to a metal tub or container and freeze for at least 6 hours before serving.

TIP

Don't panic if you boil or scramble the egg yolks – just blitz them with a stick (immersion) blender until smooth again.

Chocolate Truffles for Phillippa

MAKES
about 26 truffles

TAKES
20 minutes, plus 40 minutes chilling time

Phillippa (who you'll find tucking into toast with me on pages 64–5) is our in-house creative at Elliott's. When we're talking about the design of our coffee counter, one of the things she'll often say is, 'there's nothing better than throwing a chocolate truffle in your gob when you're grabbing coffee on the go'. Well, I couldn't agree more. So here you are Henners, my fuss-free method for indulgent truffles – not technically baking, but they always hit the spot. They're best with the grapefruit zest, but I would say that of course, I've got a thing for citrus!

---

200 ml (7 fl oz/scant 1 cup) double (heavy) cream
25 g (1 oz) butter (salted or unsalted)
pinch of sea salt flakes
200 g (7 oz) good-quality dark (bittersweet) chocolate, roughly chopped
grated zest of ⅓ grapefruit (optional)
50 g (2 oz) cocoa (unsweetened chocolate) powder, for dusting

1   Place the cream and butter in a medium saucepan over a low heat, allow the cream to bubble gently and the butter to begin to melt, then immediately remove from the heat.

2   Throw in the salt, chocolate and grapefruit zest, if using. Continue to stir until the chocolate has melted completely in the residual heat and the mixture is totally smooth.

3   Scrape the chocolate mixture into a large bowl or container and pop in the fridge for 40 minutes to firm up.

4   Meanwhile, place the cocoa (unsweetened chocolate) powder in another large, shallow bowl. Once the chocolate mixture is firm, using a spoon and your fingers, shape it into round or square truffles – I make mine into cubes around 15 g (½ oz) each, but the size and shape is up to you. As you finish shaping the truffles, toss each one in plenty of cocoa powder and set on a nice serving plate or dish.

5   These truffles keep well in an airtight container in the fridge for up to 5 days.

TIP

If at any point the chocolate ganache overheats and seizes (it looks a bit dull and grainy), stir in a splash of cold milk until smooth and glossy again. Panic over.

Evening

BAKED CRISPBREADS FOR WINE – TWO WAYS
PAGE 142

LEEK, BLUE CHEESE AND POTATO GALETTE
PAGE 146

A CRUMBLE-HEAVY CRUMBLE
PAGE 150

BURNT CHEESECAKE
PAGE 154

HAZELNUT AND BROWN SUGAR PAVLOVA
PAGE 156

MARMALADE SOURDOUGH PUDDING
PAGE 160

ELLIOTT'S FLOURLESS CHOCOLATE CAKE
PAGE 162

FIG, HAZELNUT AND CHOCOLATE CAKE
PAGE 166

Baked Crispbreads For Wine – Two Ways

MAKES
2 very large crispbreads (enough for 4 people to snack on with wine)

TAKES
15 minutes, plus 18 minutes baking time and time for making the butter

Hopefully by now you've enjoyed making the easy morning Yoghurt Flatbreads on page 54 a few times. Well, here I've given you the same dough recipe, but rather than cooking the bread in a pan, you roll it really thin and bake it in a hot oven until crisp and golden.

I've also given two different ways to flavour the crisp breads, either going with salt and vinegar vibes, or a very garlicky, herby butter. Both variations are incredible with wine and will make you really hungry for what will hopefully be a beautiful leisurely dinner ahead, in great company.

By the way, the coriander seeds aren't a must, but they do add a surprising lemony crunch.

---

125 g (4 oz/1 cup) plain (all-purpose) flour, plus extra for dusting
½ teaspoon baking powder
1½ teaspoons coriander seeds
1 teaspoon honey
125 g (4 oz) strained natural yoghurt
2 teaspoons miso paste (or ¼ teaspoon sea salt flakes if you don't have any miso in the fridge)

1 First, preheat the oven to 200°C fan (425°F/gas 7) and line 2 large baking trays (pans) with baking paper.

2 Combine the flour and baking powder in a large bowl to ensure the baking powder is evenly distributed.

3 Roughly crush the coriander seeds in a mortar with a pestle or on a cutting board with a rolling pin, then stir into the flour along with the honey, yoghurt and miso or sea salt flakes.

4 Knead the dough with your hands on a lightly-floured work surface for 1–2 minutes until smooth. Using a rolling pin dusted with flour, roll out 2 flatbreads as thinly as possible, about 32 cm (12½ in) in diameter, and transfer to the lined trays.

5 Bake in the preheated oven for 12 minutes. Carefully flip the breads over using tongs and cook for a further 6 minutes or until golden. Remove from the oven, flip again and allow to cool and crisp up while you make your chosen butter.

GARLICKY HERBY BUTTER

40 g (1½ oz) butter (salted or unsalted)
2 sprigs of rosemary, leaves only, finely chopped
6 sage leaves, finely chopped
6 garlic cloves, peeled and crushed
heavy pinch of sea salt flakes

1 Melt the butter with the herbs and garlic in a medium saucepan over a high heat for 3–4 minutes or until golden and fragrant. Remove from the heat.

2 Using a pastry brush, spread the garlicky, herby butter over the flatbreads, followed by a sprinkling of sea salt flakes.

SALT AND VINEGAR BUTTER

40 g (1½ oz) butter (salted or unsalted)
2 tablespoons cider or white wine vinegar
1 teaspoon sea salt flakes

1 Melt the butter in a medium saucepan over a high heat for 3–4 minutes or until golden. Remove from the heat and stir in the vinegar (don't worry if the butter splits slightly).

2 Using a pastry brush, spread the butter over the flatbreads, followed by a sprinkling of sea salt flakes.

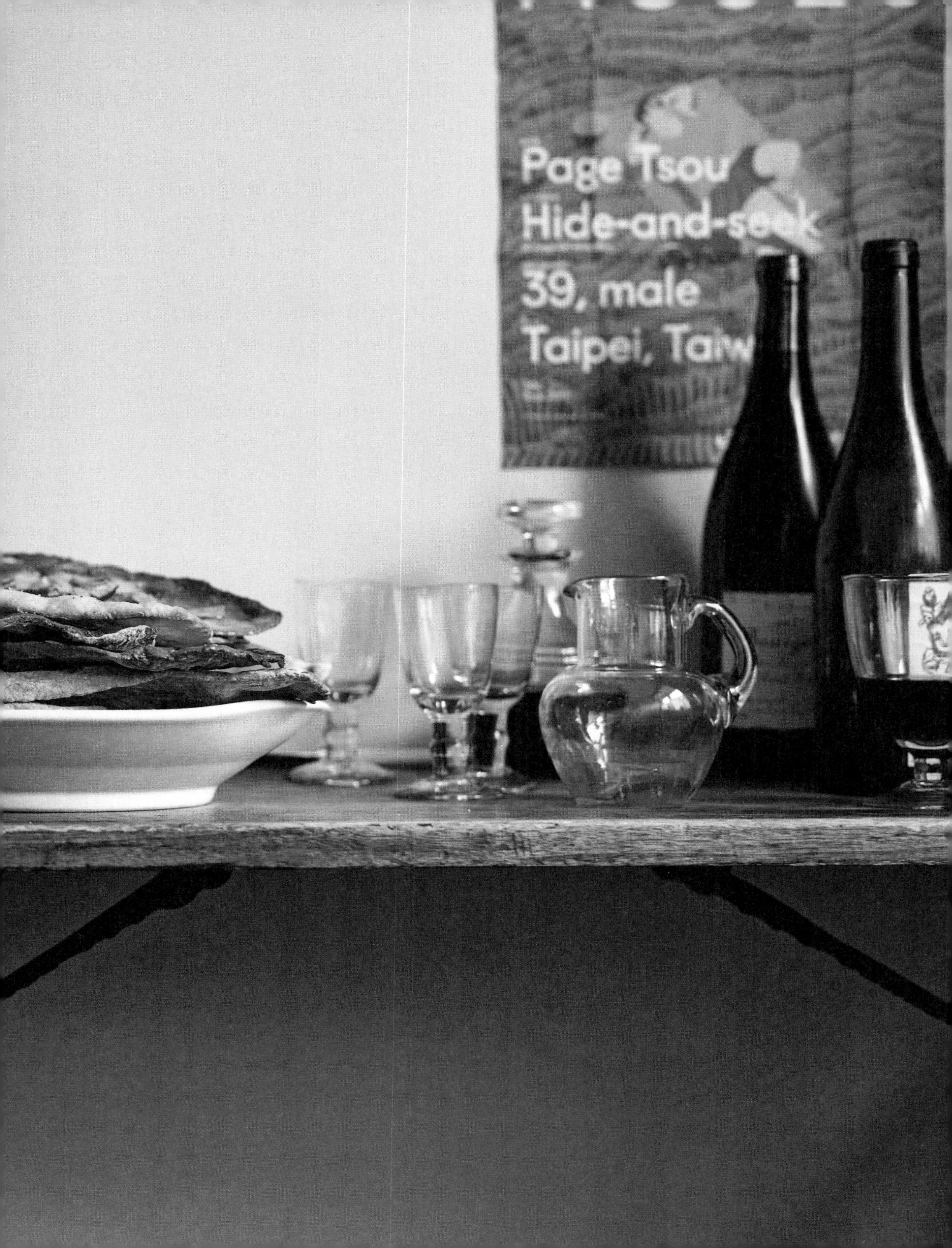
Page Tsou
Hide-and-seek
39, male
Taipei, Taiw

Leek, Blue Cheese and Potato Galette

The basic galette pastry on page 39 is a fine thing just as it is, but swap some of the plain flour for blitzed-up hazelnuts and you're onto something even more special. The nutty pastry can be made and rolled out ahead of mates coming over, so all you need to do is throw on some leeks, your favourite blue cheese and thinly sliced potatoes when they arrive.

This is a super-lazy but super-effective dinner party solution when served with a crisp salad and a lemony dressing.

SERVES
4–6

TAKES
30 minutes, plus 1 hour for chilling and 45 minutes for baking

Hazelnut pastry
50 g (2 oz) blanched hazelnuts (filberts)
pinch of sea salt flakes
100 g (3½ oz/generous ¾ cup) plain (all-purpose) flour, plus extra for dusting
85 g (3 oz) cold butter (salted or unsalted), cut into rough cubes

Galette filling
2 tablespoons cold-pressed rapeseed (canola) oil or olive oil
2 leeks, rinsed and thinly sliced
3 garlic cloves, peeled and crushed
pinch of sea salt flakes
3 baby new potatoes
75 g (2½ oz) blue cheese
½ tablespoon milk

TIP
If you don't have a food processor, finely crush the hazelnuts (filberts) in a mortar with a pestle or rolling pin. Rub together the butter and flour between your fingertips instead of pulsing in the processor.

1   First, make the pastry. Put the hazelnuts in a food processor and blitz until fine. Throw in the salt, flour and butter with a few splashes of cold water and pulse a couple of times until you get a scruffy dough. (Take care not to overwork the pastry – it's fine if you've got quite big chunks of butter.) Press the dough into a rough ball, wrap in cling film (plastic wrap) or beeswax wrap, then pop in the fridge for 1 hour, or the freezer for 30 minutes.

2   Meanwhile, make the filling. Heat the oil in a medium saucepan over a high heat. Add the leeks, garlic and salt and sweat for 5 minutes until soft but not catching. Remove from the heat.

3   Next, slice the potatoes as thinly as you safely can (use a mandoline, if you have one).

4   When the pastry has been chilling for 1 hour, preheat the oven to 200°C fan (425°F/gas 7). Lay a sheet of baking paper on your work surface and lightly it dust with flour. Roll out the pastry to a rough circle, about 28 cm (11 in) in diameter, on the floured paper. You can use a rolling pin or even a wine bottle to do this and don't worry about the pastry circle being perfectly round or neat at the edges, in fact, the scruffier the shape, the better. Transfer the pastry circle – still on the paper – to the baking tray.

5   Spread the leeks over the pastry, leaving a 2-cm (¾-in) clear border all the way round. Top with the potato slices, then break the cheese into chunks and dot over the potatoes and leeks.

6   Fold the edges of the pastry inwards to overlap the filling, pinching it slightly to create a crust. Using a pastry brush, dab the crust with milk and bake in the preheated oven for 45 minutes, or until golden and crisp at the edges. Remove from the oven and leave to cool slightly. To serve, slice the galette into 4 (as you would a pizza).

7   The galette will keep for another day when left covered, but out of the fridge. You can reheat it or enjoy it at room temperature.

A Crumble-Heavy Crumble

SERVES
6, generously

TAKES
20 minutes, plus 45 minutes
baking time

Is there anything more comforting than the smell of a crumble baking away in the oven? And, who doesn't love to peek through the glass of the oven door to witness those escapee fruit juices bubbling over onto that buttery, rubble-like crust?

While I firmly believe you shouldn't mess too much with a classic, I need more from a crumble topping than just butter, flour and sugar. I'm looking for some sort of nutty crunch, in this case flaked almonds that turn golden and crisp. A great crumble has to include some warming spices, too. But, most importantly, there's got to be plenty of it!

1 teaspoon butter, for greasing
750 g (1 lb 10 oz) apples, peeled, cored and chopped into bite-sized chunks (or use ripe pears, rhubarb stalks or any in-season fruit)
Proper Traditional Custard or Five-Minute Crème Fraîche Custard (page 27), to serve

Crumble topping
100 g (3½ oz) cold butter (salted or unsalted)
150 g (5 oz/1¼ cups) plain (all-purpose) flour
heavy pinch of sea salt flakes
½ teaspoon ground cinnamon
¼ teaspoon ground ginger
¼ teaspoon garam masala
50 g (2 oz) flaked (slivered) almonds
75 g (2½ oz) soft light brown sugar
25 g (1 oz) porridge oats
grated zest of ½ lemon

1   First, preheat the oven to 170°C fan (375°F/gas 5) and grease a deep baking dish or tin (the one I use is 20 x 25 cm/8 x 10 in) with the teaspoon of butter.

2   Throw the chopped apples into the dish, add a few splashes of water, and bake in the preheated oven for 5 minutes to get a head start on the cooked fruit.

3   Meanwhile, make the crumble topping. Using your index and middle fingers and thumbs, rub the butter, flour and salt together in a bowl until the mixture resembles rough breadcrumbs. Stir in the spices, almonds, sugar, oats and lemon zest until nicely combined. (Good luck trying not to eat the raw mixture!)

4   Remove the dish from the oven and scatter the crumble topping evenly over the apples. Return to the oven and bake for 45 minutes, or until the crumble topping is golden brown and the apples are soft. Serve while hot, ideally with a big jug of Proper Traditional Custard or Five-Minute Crème Fraîche Custard (page 27).

5   This crumble keeps well in the fridge for up to 3 days.

TIP

The crumble topping is super easy to make. The raw mixture keeps perfectly for months in the freezer, so you can always have the ingredients for a crumble on stand-by.

Burnt Cheesecake

MAKES
8 slices (23-cm (9-in) cake)

TAKES
15 minutes, plus 45–55 minutes
baking time

Impressive desserts don't really come much lazier than this rich, crust-less cheesecake. All you need to do is whisk up a handful of ingredients then blast them in a very hot oven for something that's pretty mind-blowing. You don't even need to carefully line the tin – some scrunched-up baking parchment gives the cheesecake a beautifully rustic edge.

There's a real elegance to eating this cheesecake as is, but team it with baked fruit compote (the Bay and Red Wine Blackberries on page 58, perhaps) or prunes soaked in Armagnac or whiskey if you fancy going all out.

1 tablespoon butter or oil,
   for greasing
800 g (1 lb 2 oz) cream cheese
   (ideally full-fat)
6 eggs
200 g (7 oz/generous 1 cup) caster
   (superfine) sugar
75 g (2½ oz) honey (or extra sugar
   if you don't have honey)
200 ml (7 fl oz/scant 1 cup) double
   (heavy) cream

1   First, preheat the oven to 200°C fan (425°F/gas 7) and grease the base and sides of a 23-cm (9-in) springform cake tin (pan) with the butter or oil. Line the tin with baking paper so that the paper overhangs the rim by 3 cm (1¼ in). Place the lined tin on a baking tray. (This will help you to transfer the cheesecake to and from of the oven without any spillages.)

2   Place all the remaining ingredients in a large bowl. Using a handheld electric whisk, beat everything together until smooth. (You can also use a balloon whisk or wooden spoon for this, you'll just need a bit more elbow grease!)

3   Pour the cheesecake mixture into the lined tin on the tray and bake in the preheated oven for 45–55 minutes, or until quite dark and 'burnt' on top. The cheesecake will rise like a giant, crazy soufflé but do not panic, this is exactly what you're aiming for – it will collapse back down as it cools. Leave to cool completely before serving.

4   This cheesecake keeps well in the fridge for a couple of days after baking.

TIP

Add some orange zest to the cheesecake mixture, if you like, or a little vanilla paste. It's amazing with Armagnac-soaked prunes, too.

Hazelnut and Brown Sugar Pavlova

Brown sugar brings a caramel-like quality to this foolproof meringue. Just pile it up with loads of gently whipped cream and whatever fruit you fancy and you're onto an absolute crowd-pleaser of a pudding.

Here I've used cherries, clementines and a bitter marmalade to cut through the sweetness of the meringue, but the possibilities for pav toppings are endless.

SERVES
6

TAKES
40 minutes, plus 1 hour 10 minutes baking time

---

6 egg whites (save the egg yolks for the custard recipe on page 27)
pinch of sea salt flakes
150 g (5 oz/⅔ cup) soft brown sugar
150 g (5 oz/⅔ cup) caster (superfine) sugar
50 g (2 oz) roasted hazelnuts (filberts), finely ground in a food processor
200 ml (7 fl oz/scant 1 cup) double (heavy) cream
350 g (12 oz) thick strained yoghurt
2 teaspoons honey

1 First, preheat the oven to 130°C fan (300°F/gas 2).

2 Place the egg whites and salt in a large mixing bowl. Using a handheld electric whisk, beat the egg whites to stiff peaks.

3 Combine the sugars in a bowl. Spoon one-quarter of the sugar into the egg whites and continue whisking until the sugar has fully dissolved. Repeat until all the sugar has been added.

4 Continue whisking until you can't feel any grains of sugar when rubbed between two fingers. The meringue mixture should be very glossy by this point; keep whisking, if you're not there yet.

5 Using a metal spoon, gently fold in the hazelnuts, taking care not to knock out too much of the air you've just captured in the meringue mixture.

6 Using a few blobs of meringue mixture, stick a sheet of baking paper to a baking tray (pan). Spoon the meringue mixture onto the paper to make a 25 x 30-cm (10 x 8-in) rectangle. Using the spoon, create a few peaks on the surface of the meringue.

7 Bake in the preheated oven for 1 hour 10 minutes, or until golden and crisp on the outside and slightly chewy in the middle. (Don't be tempted to open the oven door for at least 55 minutes.) Remove from the oven and leave to cool completely on the baking tray, then transfer to your favourite serving platter.

8 Meanwhile, prepare your chosen topping (see opposite).

9 Once you're ready to serve, prepare the cream. Using a handheld electric whisk, beat the cream in a bowl until soft and peaky (take care not to overwhisk or the cream can become clumpy). Fold the yoghurt into the cream, followed by the honey.

10 Spread the cream mixture over the meringue and then spoon over the scatter over your chosen topping, followed by plenty of freshly cracked black pepper.

11 The meringue (without the topping) will keep well when stored in an airtight container for a couple of days.

CHERRIES, CLEMENTINE AND MARMALADE

½ jar bitter marmalade
2 clementines
350 g (12 oz) cherries in syrup

1   Place the marmalade in a small saucepan with 2 tablespoons of water. Warm over a high heat for 2–3 minutes, stirring regularly with a wooden spoon, until you have a syrupy glaze full of orange shreds. Remove from the heat and allow to cool completely.

2   Use a microplane or fine side of a box grater to zest 1 of the clementines. Then cut away the skin and peel from both clementines and slice into segments.

3   Spoon cooled marmalade over the whipped cream, followed by the clementine segments and cherries. Sprinkle over the zest to finish.

BLACKBERRIES, RED WINE AND BLACK PEPPER

300 g (10½ oz) blackberries
2 tablespoons red wine
freshly cracked black pepper

1   Toss the blackberries with the red wine in a small bowl and allow to sit for at least 20 minutes.

2   Spoon over the whipped cream followed by plenty of freshly-ground black pepper.

STRAWBERRIES, LEMON CURD AND MINT

250 g (9 oz) good-quality lemon curd
400 g (14 oz) strawberries, hulled and halved
a few stalks of mint (5 g/½ oz)

1   Blob spoonfuls of the lemon curd over the whipped cream.

2   Scatter over the strawberries, then tear over the mint leaves to finish.

Marmalade Sourdough Pudding

SERVES
6–8 (with plenty of leftovers to get you through the start of the week)

TAKES
15 minutes, plus 30–35 minutes baking time

Whenever you're in need of comfort on a Sunday afternoon, I urge you to try this super-easy sponge pudding. The sourdough brings an interesting texture and savoury flavour to the sponge, and the sticky bittersweet marmalade offers complete nostalgia with that homely smell of marmalade on toast.

Just add a splash of cold cream or jug of Proper Traditional Custard (page 27), then quietly fall into a nap on the couch.

250 g (9 oz) butter (salted or unsalted), soft/at room temperature, plus 1 teaspoon for greasing
100 g (3½ oz) leftover sourdough bread (crusts removed before weighing) – about 2 thick slices
220-g (7¾-oz) jar of marmalade (my favourite is the Seville orange and chamomile marmalade made by London Borough of Jam)
150 g (5 oz/generous ¾ cup) light soft brown sugar
150 g (5 oz/1¼ cups) plain (all-purpose) flour
½ teaspoon bicarbonate of soda (baking soda)
1 teaspoon baking powder
4 eggs, cracked into a small bowl
pinch of sea salt flakes
jug (pitcher) of double (heavy) cream, to serve (optional)

1 First, preheat the oven to 180°C (400°F/gas 6) and grease the base and sides of a large baking dish with the teaspoon of butter. (Any large ovenproof dish will work – I like to use a 23-cm/9-in paella pan from Brindisa.)

2 Next, cut the bread into rough chunks, place in a food processor and blitz to fine breadcrumbs. Add the remaining butter, two-thirds of the marmalade, sugar, flour, bicarbonate of soda, baking powder, eggs and salt and pulse until combined. (You can carefully use a box grater to crush the bread into crumbs and then beat everything with a wooden spoon in a large bowl until smooth).

3 Using a silicone spatula or wooden spoon, scrape the batter into the buttered dish and bake in the preheated oven for 30–35 minutes, or until deep golden. Remove from the oven and leave to cool slightly in the dish.

4 Meanwhile, place the remaining marmalade in a small saucepan with 2 tablespoons of water. Warm over a high heat for 2–3 minutes, stirring regularly with a wooden spoon, until you have a syrupy glaze full of orange shreds.

5 Pour the marmalade glaze over the top of the sponge, allow it to sink in for a minute or two, then serve the pudding – ideally with plenty of cold double cream.

TIP

If there are less than 6 people to feed, you can easily halve the quantities in this recipes and bake the pudding in a smaller dish, which is what I've done in the photo opposite.

Elliott's Flourless Chocolate Cake

MAKES
8 slices (23-cm (9-in) cake)

TAKES
25 minutes, plus 45 minutes
baking time

From day one this has been our top-seller at Elliott's, so I'm almost embarrassed to share just how easily you can recreate it at home. Simply melt chocolate and butter in a pan, throw in salt, sugar, cocoa and eggs and, after some time in the oven, you're onto the richest, fudgiest most crowd-pleasing pudding ever.

I've discovered that the chocolate cake tastes incredible when frozen too – think chocolate fudge brownie ice cream, but lazier!

200 g (7 oz) dark (bittersweet) chocolate, coarsely chopped
200 g (7 oz) butter (salted or unsalted), plus 1 tablespoon for greasing
½ teaspoon sea salt flakes
250 g (9 oz/1⅓ cups) soft brown sugar (light or dark brown work equally well)
70 g (2½ oz/generous ½ cup) cocoa (unsweetened chocolate) powder, plus 2 tablespoons for dusting
6 eggs

1   First, gently melt the chocolate and butter with the salt in a large, high-sided saucepan over a low heat. At the point of being almost melted, remove from the heat – the chocolate and butter will continue to melt in the residual heat.

2   Next, preheat the oven to 180°C fan (400°F/gas 6) and use the extra tablespoon of butter to grease a 23-cm (9-in) springform cake tin (pan), then line the base and sides with baking paper.

3   Using a balloon whisk, stir the sugar and cocoa (unsweetened chocolate) powder into the chocolate mixture – by this point, it should be a comfortable enough temperature for you to dip your finger into. Crack in the eggs and continue to whisk until smooth and glossy.

4   Scrape the batter into the lined tin and bake in the preheated oven for 45 minutes, or until the cake has risen slightly. Remove from the oven. At this point the cake will collapse slightly and become all truffle-y and rich! Allow to cool completely then using a small sieve (strainer), dust with the extra cocoa powder.

5   This cake keeps well in the fridge for up to 5 days and is ridiculously good served with strained natural yoghurt.

Fig, Hazelnut and Chocolate Cake

MAKES
8 slices (23-cm (9-in) cake)

TAKES
25 minutes, plus 40–45 minutes
baking time

This is a very special, indulgent cake, which is why I make it around Christmas time. It's the kind of cake that keeps well for a good few days in a tin, so it is ideal for serving to any visiting guests.

Thanks to the ground almonds, you've got a squidgy sponge with underlying hints of spice from the vanilla, black pepper and ground coriander, chunks of dark chocolate, toasted hazelnuts, then some festive, warming booze thanks to the brandy-soaked figs. If alcohol isn't your thing, just soak the figs in some Earl Grey or breakfast tea instead – the cake will taste just as amazing.

---

250 g (9 oz) unsalted butter, soft/ at room temperature, cut into rough cubes, plus 2 teaspoons for greasing

200 g (7 oz) dried figs, finely chopped

4 tablespoons Armagnac, rum, amaretto or whiskey (optional)

250 g (9 oz/generous 1 cup) caster (superfine) sugar

4 large eggs

1 teaspoon vanilla paste

20 turns of black pepper

3 teaspoons ground coriander

75 g (2½ oz) plain (all-purpose) flour (substitute with extra ground almonds if you prefer the cake to be gluten-free)

100 g (3½ oz) ground almonds

100 g (3½ oz) dark (bittersweet) chocolate, minimum 60% cocoa solids, finely chopped

75 g (3½ oz) blanched hazelnuts (filberts), bashed or coarsely chopped

---

1   First, preheat the oven to 180°C fan (400°F/gas 6) and grease a 23-cm (9-in) springform cake tin (pan) with the 2 teaspoons of butter. Line the base and sides of the tin with baking paper.

2   Place the chopped figs in a small bowl with the Armagnac or other alcohol of your choice, if using.

3   Using a handheld electric whisk in a large mixing bowl (or a wooden spoon and lots of muscle), cream together the butter and sugar until pale and fluffy. Crack in the eggs, one at a time, beating well between each addition.

4   Next, stir in the vanilla paste, pepper and coriander. If the mixture curdles, don't worry, just whisk in 1 tablespoon of the flour.

5   Fold in the flour, ground almonds, chocolate, figs and Armagnac, then stir until just combined.

6   Scrape the batter into the lined tin. Sprinkle over the hazelnuts and then, using a wooden spoon, lightly push them into the surface of the cake. Bake in the preheated oven for 40–45 minutes until golden. A skewer or knife inserted into the middle of the cake should come out clean (apart from some melted chocolate). Leave to cool in the tin before removing and slicing.

7   This cake keeps well in an airtight container for up to 4 days.

ABOUT JESS

Raised in East London by hungry and adventurous parents, Jess has always been obsessed with good food and simple cooking.

Being a self-taught cook, her route into a career in food has been pretty unconventional. A job in marketing and product development with Jamie Oliver introduced Jess to the world of recipe writing and food styling, leading her to write *Salad Feasts* and *Tin Can Magic*, alongside working on commercials, cookery shows and for magazines.

Her relaxed, everyday approach to cooking is influenced by warm childhood memories of eating with family and delicious times spent living in Bangkok, Sydney and London.

Jess opened Elliott's as an excuse to make feeding people while having a good chat her main job, alongside writing her books.

ABOUT ELLIOTT'S

Founded by Jess in 2018, Elliott's is a much-loved community that celebrates simple cooking and everyday life in the kitchen.

Based in Edinburgh, the Elliott's Kitchen and Workshop are just a few doors down from each other on Sciennes Road. Elliott's Kitchen at number 27 is the go-to place to drink good coffee, enjoy lunch and stock up on store-cupboard ingredients. There, Jess and her team make pickles and jams, proper cakes, seasonal drinks and food that makes everyone happy. You can buy some good stuff to take home for dinner along with a bottle of wine, then enjoy a natter on the orange benches out front.

The Workshop along the road at number 21 is Elliott's creative space. It's where Jess develops ideas and writes recipes and where the art department curate, design and make fun things. It's also home to the popular Elliott's online store.

@elliottsedinburgh

OVEN TEMPERATURES

Gas	°F	°C	Fan °C	Gas	°F	°C	Fan °C
1	275	140	120	6	400	200	180
2	300	150	130	7	425	220	200
3	325	160	140	8	450	230	210
4	350	180	160	9	475	240	220
5	375	190	170	10	500	260	240

INDEX

A

almonds
  apple frangipane galette 82
  basic frangipane 45–7
  fennel seed and lemon pastries 70
  miso-honey almond butter 63
  seasonal fruit friands 96
  soft amaretti 80
  thumbprint cookies 94
  yoghurt cake 89
amaretti: soft amaretti 80
apples
  apple and cardamom jam 33
  apple frangipane galette 82

B

biscuits
  Elliott's sea salt chocolate
    cookies 116
  one-jar peanut butter cookies 126
  peanut butter and chocolate
    cookies 126
  peanut butter and jam cookies 126
  soft amaretti 80
  thumbprint cookies 94
blackberries, red wine and black
  pepper pavlova 157
blackberries: bay and red wine
  blackberries 58
blackcurrants: Yorkshire pudding
  pancake 60
blue cheese: leek, blue cheese and
  potato galette 146
blueberry and rosemary jam 33
bread
  baked crispbreads for wine
    – two ways 142
  marmalade sourdough pudding 160
  porridge soda bread rolls 52
  sage, garlic and cheese loaf for
    soup 108
  yoghurt flatbreads 54–6
  yoghurt flatbreads with dill-
    scrambled eggs & yoghurt 55
butter 17

C

cakes
  cake for coffee 77
  Elliott's flourless chocolate
    cake 162
  fig, hazelnut and chocolate
    cake 166
  grapefruit drizzle loaf 124
  jam and coconut sponge 115
  lemon Earl-Grey polenta loaf 84
  Marmite brownies 121
  my go-to brown sugar sponge
    (with seasonal fruit) 128
  olive oil, chocolate and orange
    loaf 134
  seasonal fruit friands 96
  sticky triple ginger cake 131
  sugar buns for tea 132
  yoghurt cake 89
cardamom: apple and cardamom
  jam 33
Cheddar
  Cheddar and mustard scones 109
  sage, garlic and cheese loaf
    for soup 108
cheese
  burnt cheesecake 154
  Cheddar and mustard scones 109
  leek, blue cheese and potato
    galette 146
  sage, garlic and cheese loaf
    for soup 108
  spinach, dill and feta filo pies 90
  tomato, parmesan and caper
    galettes 104
cheesecake: burnt cheesecake 154
cherries, clementine and marmalade
  pavlova 157
chicken curry pie 112
chocolate
  chocolate truffles for Phillippa 139
  Elliott's flourless chocolate cake 162
  Elliott's sea salt chocolate
    cookies 116
  fig, hazelnut and chocolate cake 166
  Marmite brownies 121
  olive oil, chocolate and orange
    loaf 134
  peanut butter and chocolate
    cookies 126
  salted chocolate hazelnut
    spread 63

citrus fruit
  cake for coffee 77
  soft amaretti 80
clementines: cherries, clementine and marmalade pavlova 157
cookies. *see* biscuits
cream
  chocolate truffles for Phillippa 139
  proper traditional custard 27
cream cheese: burnt cheesecake 154
crème fraîche
  five-minute crème fraîche custard 27
  no-churn crème fraîche ice cream 27, 136
crispbread: baked crispbreads for wine 142
curries: chicken curry pie 112
custard 27–9
  five-minute crème fraîche custard 27
  proper traditional custard 27

D

desserts
  blackberries, red wine and black pepper pavlova 157
  burnt cheesecake 154
  cherries, clementine and marmalade pavlova 157
  a crumble heavy crumble 150
  hazelnut and brown sugar pavlova 156
  jam and coconut sponge 115
  marmalade sourdough pudding 160
  strawberries, lemon curd and mint pavlova 157

E

Earl Grey tea: lemon Earl-Grey polenta loaf 84
eggs 17
  one-cup pancakes 67
  yoghurt flatbreads with dill-scrambled eggs & yoghurt 55
  yoghurt flatbreads with sage-fried eggs & lemony greens 56
  Yorkshire pudding pancake 60
equipment 14–16

F

fennel seed and lemon pastries 70
feta: spinach, dill and feta filo pies 90
figs
  fig, hazelnut and chocolate cake 166
  yoghurt flatbreads with crushed coriander seeds, honey & figs 56
filo pastry: spinach, dill and feta filo pies 90
flatbreads
  yoghurt flatbreads 54
  yoghurt flatbreads with crushed coriander seeds, honey & figs 56
  yoghurt flatbreads with dill-scrambled eggs & yoghurt 55
  yoghurt flatbreads with sage-fried eggs & lemony greens 56
frangipane
  apple frangipane galette 82
  basic frangipane 45–7
  fennel seed and lemon pastries 70
fruit
  a crumble heavy crumble 150
  my go-to brown sugar sponge (with seasonal fruit) 128
  seasonal fruit friands 96

G

galettes 37, 40
  apple frangipane galette 82
  leek, blue cheese and potato galette 146
  tomato, parmesan and caper galettes 104
ginger
  rhubarb and ginger jam 33
  sticky triple ginger cake 131
grapefruit
  cake for coffee 77
  grapefruit drizzle loaf 124

H

hazelnuts
  fig, hazelnut and chocolate cake 166
  hazelnut and brown sugar pavlova 156
  leek, blue cheese and potato galette 146
  salted chocolate hazelnut spread 63

I

ice cream: no-churn crème fraîche ice cream 136

J

jam 33–5
  apple and cardamom jam 33
  blueberry and rosemary jam 33
  jam and coconut sponge 115
  peanut butter and jam cookies 126
  rhubarb and ginger jam 33
  strawberry and lemon jam 33
  thumbprint cookies 94

L

leek, blue cheese and potato galette 146
lemon curd: strawberries, lemon curd and mint pavlova 157
lemons 21
  cake for coffee 77
  fennel seed and lemon pastries 70
  lemon Earl-Grey polenta loaf 84
  seasonal fruit friands 96
  strawberry and lemon jam 33
  yoghurt cake 89

M

marmalade sourdough pudding 160
Marmite brownies 121
meringues
  blackberries, red wine and black pepper pavlova 157
  cherries, clementine and marmalade pavlova 157
  hazelnut and brown sugar pavlova 156
  strawberries, lemon curd and mint pavlova 157
milk 17
  one-cup pancakes 67
  proper traditional custard 27
  Yorkshire pudding pancake 60

miso paste 20
  baked crispbreads for wine 142
  miso-honey almond butter 63
  yoghurt flatbreads 54–6

N

nuts: basic frangipane 45–7

O

oats: porridge soda bread rolls 52
oranges: olive oil, chocolate and orange loaf 134

P

pancakes
  one-cup pancakes 67
  Yorkshire pudding pancake 60
parmesan: tomato, parmesan and caper galettes 104
pastries. *see also* galettes
  fennel seed and lemon pastries 70
  pork and fennel sausage rolls 102
  spinach,dill and feta filo pies 90
  tomato, parmesan and caper galettes 104
pastry 21
  basic pastry 39–41
peanut butter: one-jar peanut butter cookies 126
pies: chicken curry pie 112
polenta: lemon Earl-Grey polenta loaf 84
puff pastry 21
  fennel seed and lemon pastries 70
  pork and fennel sausage rolls 102

R

rhubarb and ginger jam 33
rolls: porridge soda bread rolls 52
rosemary: blueberry and rosemary jam 33

S

sausage rolls: pork and fennel sausage rolls 102
scones: Cheddar and mustard scones 109
spinach, dill and feta filo pies 90
spreads 63
  miso-honey almond butter 63
  salted chocolate hazelnut spread 63
storecupboard essentials 20
strawberries
  strawberries, lemon curd and mint pavlova 157
  strawberry and lemon jam 33

T

toast: spreads for toast 63
tomato, parmesan and caper galettes 104
truffles: chocolate truffles for Phillippa 139

V

vanilla 17

W

wine: bay and red wine blackberries 58

Y

yoghurt
  cake for coffee 77
  porridge soda bread rolls 52
  yoghurt cake 89
  yoghurt flatbreads 54–6
Yorkshire pudding pancake 60

Published in 2021 by Hardie Grant Books,
an imprint of Hardie Grant Publishing

Hardie Grant Books (London)
5th & 6th Floors
52–54 Southwark Street
London SE1 1UN

Hardie Grant Books (Melbourne)
Building 1, 658 Church Street
Richmond, Victoria 3121

hardiegrantbooks.com

British Library Cataloguing-in-Publication Data. A catalogue
record for this book is available from the British Library.

Lazy Baking
ISBN: 978-1-78488-433-8

10 9 8 7 6 5 4 3 2 1

Publisher and Commissioner: Kajal Mistry
Editor: Eila Purvis
Designers: Evi-O.Studio | Nicole Ho, Wilson Leung, Evi O.
Photographer: Matt Russell
Food Stylist: Jessica Elliott Dennison
Creative direction: Phillippa Henley
Copy-editor: Laura Nickoll
Proofreader: Lisa Pendreigh
Indexer: Cathy Heath
Production Controller: Sabeena Atchia

Colour reproduction by p2d
Printed and bound in China by Leo Paper Products Ltd.